CH00764458

This book is an absolute must-read for anyone in Christi[...] [...]lical, it will both help you personally and have a profoundly p[...] [...]rs. Get hold of a copy today and put the wisdom pouring out [...]

GAVIN CALVER, CEO, EVANGELICAL ALLIANC[...]

This book contains fifty-two short and sharp resources, providing a thesaurus on Christian leadership and wisdom and a toolkit for leaders to use with others in exploration, faith building, learning and growth. Diagrams help to explain complexity simply, clearly and concisely. This could be the most useful Christian leadership reference book ever!

JILL GARRETT, EXECUTIVE DIRECTOR, TENTPEG CONSULTING; AUTHOR AND CONTRIBUTOR, *OXFORD HANDBOOK OF POSITIVE PSYCHOLOGY* AND *NEW FORMS OF LOCAL GOVERNANCE*; PODCAST PRODUCER, *GOBSTOPPER*

There are two remarkable things about this book: The first is that it distils an entire library of wisdom into fifty-two simple summaries. The second – and most remarkable – is that these distillations of truth are given as diagrams. These diagrams have many of the virtues of Jesus' parables: They provoke our interaction, force us into thinking about their meaning and, finally, lodge deeply and firmly in our brains. Fifty-two summaries about life and leadership. That's a year's subscription to some unforgettable weekly lessons.

CANON J.JOHN, EVANGELIST, SPEAKER AND AUTHOR

If a well-constructed diagram makes the tool immediately understandable and eminently doable, then this book is bound to make a big impact on your life. It is a treasure trove of concentrated leadership wisdom. Highly recommended.

ALAN HIRSCH, AUTHOR OF NUMEROUS BOOKS ON MISSIONAL THEOLOGY, SPIRITUALITY, LEADERSHIP, AND ORGANISATION; FOUNDER, MOVEMENT LEADERS COLLECTIVE, THE 5Q COLLECTIVE AND FORGE MISSIONAL TRAINING NETWORK

Leadiagrams is a goldmine of leadership nuggets captured in one book! I have hundreds of books on my bookshelves and too frequently scramble to find a diagram or leadership concept floating about in my mind. No longer. *Leadiagrams* will now be the first place I go. The Frost brothers serve up a rich compilation of renowned leadership principles that are immensely practical and designed to accelerate your leadership. What a gift for those of us who lead.

DR CRAIG SIDER, FOUNDER, INFOCUS LEADERSHIP

Andy and Chris Frost have written a remarkable book on leadership formation and practice that will be invaluable for leaders globally. The book provides a tremendous road map for personal, church and organisational leadership – a great read and annual re-read.

DR MAC PIER, FOUNDER, MOVEMENT.ORG

A great resource for learning how to lead others – and *yourself*!

ROB PARSONS OBE, FOUNDER AND CHAIRMAN, CARE FOR THE FAMILY; AUTHOR, *THE HEART OF SUCCESS*

So simple yet so incredibly helpful – one read of *Leadiagrams* has already strengthened my leadership, and this is a brilliant tool I am going to refer to time and time again. It has helped and will help me to become a more resilient leader, but more importantly it will help me and other leaders I know to raise resilient leaders too. I'll be recommending it to every leader I know!

NATALIE WILLIAMS, CHIEF EXECUTIVE, JUBILEE+

In the complexity of life, you must balance your faith, work, health and sanity. If you've ever wondered 'how it all fits together', for those who believe in the God who created everything in holistic balance, *Leadiagrams* serves as a visual key to understanding life's puzzle.

PEYTON JONES, FOUNDER, NEWBREED TRAINING, SAN DIEGO; TRAINING DIRECTOR, THE MXPLATFORM; AUTHOR, *CHURCH PLANTOLOGY: THE ART AND SCIENCE OF PLANTING CHURCHES; REACHING THE UNREACHED: BECOMING RAIDERS OF THE LOST ARK;* AND *CHURCH ZERO: RAISING 1ST CENTURY CHURCHES OUT OF THE ASHES OF THE 21ST CENTURY*

Why has no-one thought of producing something like this before? I LOVE this book, which will become a part of my leadership toolkit. It's jam-packed with a fleet of creative tools and models to help spark catalytic development conversations with your team members.

MATT SUMMERFIELD, SENIOR PASTOR, ZEO CHURCH, WWW.ZEOCHURCH. COM; COACH AND TRAINER, WWW.STRETCH-YOUR-LIFE.COM; EX-CEO AND PRESIDENT, URBAN SAINTS

Leadiagrams has been expertly curated to gather tried and tested, effective and insightful concepts in a user-friendly and accessible format. It will inform, inspire and equip you as a leader and is a vital resource to release potential in ourselves, others and the projects we lead.

RICH ROBINSON, LEADER, MOVEMENT LEADERS COLLECTIVE AND CREO; FOUNDER, CATALYSE CHANGE

In *Leadiagrams*, Andy and Chris have done a great job in compiling much of the best wisdom around, enabling leaders and churches to flourish. Their engaging and practical style makes this a very accessible resource – a great starting point, whatever challenge or opportunity you are currently facing.

CHARLES GLASS, BUSINESS COACH TO COMMERCIAL, CHARITABLE AND CHURCH LEADERS; TRUSTEE, NEWFRONTIERS INTERNATIONAL TRUST

Many leaders are looking for ways to communicate what they are thinking or what they want to achieve, but often over complicate things because they can't find the words. This book is a treasure trove of leadership nuggets, simplified into diagrams that will help any leader in any setting to communicate principal concepts that are both provoking and appliable. Whether you are working in a church or business setting, this is a must read for any leader.

ANDREW J. SWIFT, CHIEF PROCUREMENT OFFICER, BRITISH COUNCIL; AUTHOR, *MY REASON FOR HOPE AND THIS PAGE LEFT BLANK?: FULFILLING YOUR DREAMS*

I love diagrams that help me explain and understand concepts, models and approaches. Simple visual pictures that I can use and more easily remember. What a treat to find a whole book with fifty-two of them!

REVD ROGER SUTTON, CO CEO, GATHER MOVEMENT; FORMER PASTOR, ALTRINCHAM BAPTIST CHURCH MANCHESTER, UK; AUTHOR, *GATHERING MOMENTUM*

As a scientist I love and live diagrams and visuals – and in this book they are used by people with vast experience of leadership in many contexts. Whether you're starting out on your leadership journey or still learning, this is an invaluable resource for forming and equipping Christian leaders.

REVD PROFESSOR DAVID WILKINSON, PRINCIPAL, ST JOHN'S COLLEGE, DURHAM UNIVERSITY

Powerful. Succinct. Personal. Penetrating. Andy and Chris draw upon transformational stories, their life experiences and influential leaders to equip their readers to live a more robust and meaningful life. From leading yourself to leading others, to discussing your destiny or the 'snakes and ladders' in your context, *Leadiagrams* will help you live a more authentic, satisfying and influential life.

DR WES GRIFFIN, PRESIDENT AND CEO, INTERNATIONAL LEADERSHIP INSTITUTE, ILITEAM.ORG

It is past time to shift the way we think and lead. This book will help us. Using imagery and right-side brain power to fuel inspiration, curiosity and possibility – you will love it.

DANIELLE STRICKLAND, ADVOCATE, AUTHOR AND SPEAKER.

Leadiagrams

52 VISUALS TO HELP YOU THRIVE IN YOUR FAITH AND LEAD EFFECTIVELY

ANDY FROST & CHRIS FROST

100 MOVEMENTS
PUBLISHING

First published in 2023 by 100 Movements Publishing

www.100Mpublishing.com

Copyright © 2023 by Andy Frost and Chris Frost

All rights reserved. No portion of this book may be reproduced or transmitted in any form or by any means, electronic or mechanical, including photocopying, recording, or by any information storage and retrieval system, without permission in writing from the authors. The only exception is brief quotations in printed reviews.

The authors have no responsibility for the persistence or accuracy of URLs for external or third-party internet websites referred to in this book, and do not guarantee that any content on such websites is, or will remain, accurate or appropriate.

All Scripture quotations, unless otherwise indicated, are taken from The Holy Bible, New International Version® NIV® Copyright © 1973 1978 1984 2011 by Biblica, Inc.™ Used by permission. All rights reserved worldwide.

Scripture quotations marked CEV are taken from the Contemporary English Version® Copyright © 1995 American Bible Society. All rights reserved.

Scripture quotations marked ESV are taken from the ESV® Bible (The Holy Bible, English Standard Version®). ESV® Text Edition: 2016. Copyright © 2001 by Crossway, a publishing ministry of Good News Publishers. The ESV® text has been reproduced in cooperation with and by permission of Good News Publishers. Unauthorized reproduction of this publication is prohibited. All rights reserved.

Scripture quotations marked NASB are taking form the New American Standard Bible®, Copyright © 1960, 1971, 1977, 1995 by The Lockman Foundation. All rights reserved.
The "NASB," "NAS," "New American Standard Bible," and "New American Standard," are trademarks registered in the United States Patent and Trademark Office by The Lockman Foundation. Use of these trademarks requires the permission of The Lockman Foundation.

Scripture quotations marked NLT are taken from the Holy Bible, New Living Translation, copyright ©1996, 2004, 2015 by Tyndale House Foundation. Used by permission of Tyndale House Publishers, Carol Stream, Illinois 60188. All rights reserved.

See page 237 for diagram credits.

ISBN 978-1-955142-35-9 (print)

Cover design and illustrations by Daniel Watson Design.

www.danielwatsondesign.co.uk

100 Movements Publishing

An imprint of Movement Leaders Collective

Cody, Wyoming

www.movementleaderscollective.com

www.catalysechange.org

*For all those leaders who made
sacrifices to help us grow as leaders.*

Contents

LEADING
YOURSELF

SECTION 2: **LEADING OTHERS**

Leading Others with *Understanding*:
Diagrams for Discerning the Heart of Others

Leading Others with *Communication*:
Diagrams for Expressing Your Heart to Others

Leading Others in *Synergy*:
Diagrams for Achieving Collaboration

SECTION 3: **LEADING PROJECTS** 123

Leading Projects _Internally_:
Diagrams for Effective Internal Approaches

Leading Projects _Externally_:
Diagrams for Effective External Approaches

Leading Projects _Holistically_:
Diagrams for Effective Change

SECTION 4: **LEADING CHURCH LIFE** 177

Introduction

If a picture paints a thousand words, just imagine what a properly understood diagram can do. In our visually based and time-poor culture, leaders need simple, shareable and globally applicable tools that will equip them in every sphere of life. This book is crammed with fifty-two big and memorable ideas to help you thrive in your faith and lead effectively, whether in your community, your workplace or in Christian ministry.

Through a combined forty-plus years of Christian leadership in over twenty nations, alongside three master's degrees on the subject, we have collated these diagrams from our distinct experiences, as well as from leading thinkers in emotional and spiritual health, theology, business and mission.

HOW TO USE THIS BOOK

The diagrams are split into four sections: Leading Yourself, Leading Others, Leading Projects and Leading Church Life.

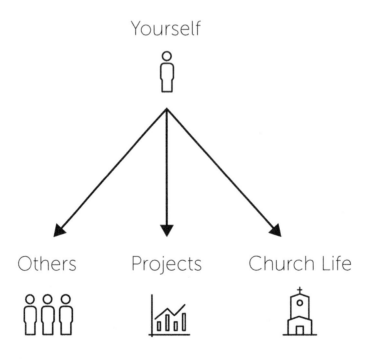

Each of these four sections is broken down further into three tailored subsections. This enables you to follow a mapped-out journey through the book, or alternatively to pick out a specific area you want to focus on.

Each diagram is unpacked in segments:

- **Setting the Scene** – providing a context for understanding the significance of the diagram.
- **What's the Big Idea?** – explaining the main concept that the diagram summarises.
- **Thinking Biblically** – applying a biblical lens through which to understand the diagram.
- **How Do I Apply It?** – outlining how you can practically implement the idea.
- **Questions for Reflection** – provoking you towards further personal thought.
- **Go Further** – signposting towards the original or related material for deeper understanding.

There are a number of contexts in which you might use this book:

PERSONALLY

As leaders we need to keep sharp and be aware of our own blind spots. The diagrams in the book can be used for personal reflection, providing a year's worth of weekly, five-minute opportunities to invest in sharpening your thinking. The Questions for Reflection could be journalled and become a part of your devotional life as you invite God to help you lead well.

MENTORING OTHERS

Over the years, these diagrams have been helpful for us as we have mentored and encouraged others in a one-to-one situation. You could either work through a selection of the diagrams applicable to the person you are mentoring or use them in a more ad hoc way. For example, if someone comes to you looking for advice on how to manage a colleague, how to discern their calling, or how they can create a better work/life balance, reach for this book and find the appropriate diagram. These versatile diagrams will become valuable tools in your belt that will help you to mentor and coach others.

LEADING TEAMS

Many of us will have the regular task of chairing, or participating in, team meetings. The diagrams in this book are easy to redraw on a whiteboard or on a piece of paper and provide some quick-to-explain ideas that can help a team grasp a big idea and shape a response to the challenges and opportunities they may be facing. Over the years, we have used the diagrams in church leadership teams, in community stakeholder meetings, in business workshops and as trustees in the charitable sector. We have also found that many of the diagrams can be used off the cuff, drawn from memory when a specific issue arises.

SHARING MORE WIDELY

Whether you are speaking to a congregation on a Sunday morning or enthusing your colleagues on a Monday morning, these diagrams are a great added extra for presentations. They can offer a practical application to a sermon or can help illustrate a business or third-sector presentation.

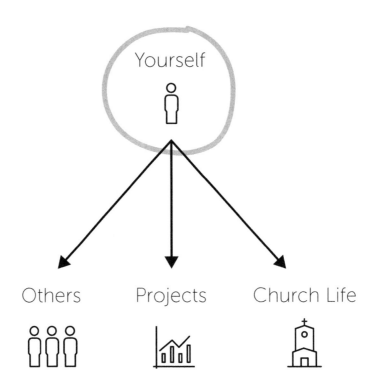

Section 1

LEADING YOURSELF

The hardest person to lead will always be you. Faking it just won't cut it because Jesus taught us to lead authentically from the inside out. This challenge can only be faced effectively when we are not just God-aware but also self-aware. Therefore, the first thirteen diagrams start where leadership should start: from the inside out.

LEADING YOURSELF **UPWARDLY**:
Diagrams for Relating with God

1. Grasping Acceptance: The Cycle of Grace
2. Holistic Spirituality: The Heart, Head, Hands and Huddle Triangle
3. Knowing God: Divine Connections
4. Strategic Praying: The Handy Prayer Tool

LEADING YOURSELF **INWARDLY**:
Diagrams for Your Internal World

5. Performing Well: The Emotional Energy Matrix
6. Getting to Know Yourself: The Johari Window
7. Going Deeper: The Iceberg of Emotional Health
8. Feel the Feelings: The Emotions Wheel

LEADING YOURSELF **OUTWARDLY**:
Diagrams for Time and Relationships

9. Intentional Connectedness: The Spiritual Growth Network
10. Out of the Comfort Zone: The Challenge Graph
11. First Things First: The Priority Jar
12. Holding on to Hope: The Circles of Pressure
13. Discerning Calling: The Sweet Spot

Grasping Acceptance

THE CYCLE OF GRACE

CHRIS

The Cycle of Grace

ACCEPTANCE · SUSTENANCE · SIGNIFICANCE · ACHIEVEMENT

The Cycle of Works

ACHIEVEMENT · ACCEPTANCE · SUSTENANCE · SIGNIFICANCE

SETTING THE SCENE

Have you ever lost your keys?

The last time I lost mine, I remember the agitation intensifying as the search continued and the growing dread of the consequences started to play out in my head: I'll be late for my meeting … I'll have to get new keys cut! I then unleashed my internal dialogue on my family, accusingly: 'Who's moved my keys?'

Almost as suddenly as the panic started, a jangle as I moved my leg revealed the embarrassing fact that the keys were in my pocket all along! Relief flowed over me, and an apology was issued to my family.

Like searching for a lost set of keys, we often search frantically for acceptance, but the truth is, as followers of Jesus we already have more than we could ever dream of through the gospel. It's in our pockets all along, but it doesn't stop us searching.

In the original *Rocky* movie, Rocky Balboa is facing his big fight with Apollo Creed. The arduous training is complete, and talking with his wife, Adrian, the night before the battle, he gruffly says, 'All I wanna do is go the distance. No one's ever gone the distance with Creed, and if I can go that distance … I'll know for the first time in my life that I weren't just another bum from the neighborhood.'

Script writers create scenes like that because they know they connect with the universal and unceasing ache of the human heart. Everyone longs for acceptance; we desperately search for something to prove that we're not just 'another bum'.

Your search for acceptance is unlikely to be found through winning a physical fight, but you probably put hope into other potential successes, with the expectation that they will result in acceptance. The litmus is often the strength of your emotional reaction to any failure of one of these hopes. Imagine Rocky being defeated by Apollo. Imagine never gaining what you have great hope for.

WHAT'S THE BIG IDEA?

The Cycle of Grace starts with Acceptance. If you've accepted the gospel, you're accepted by God because of the work of Jesus. Therefore, you are completely and fully accepted by God just as you are; not the better version of you, the one you wish you were. Even with all of your faults and failings – past, present and future – you are accepted. Pause and let that sink in a moment ... what beautiful grace!

Then the cycle moves to Sustenance. The awareness of your Acceptance produces in you the essential spiritual nutrients of a consistent love.

This Sustenance works powerfully in you to create a clear sense of Significance, where you're assured that not only are you loved by the Son, but because of your adoption by God, you *are* a son or daughter of God!

This in turn makes you ready for Achievement; you're not doing activity *for* Significance, which can get you burned out, but *from* the Significance you already have in Christ.

And so the cycle continues. If what you achieve is seemingly fruitful or fruitless, it ultimately doesn't matter, because your Acceptance is based upon what Jesus has done for you, not what you do for him.

This is powerful stuff, but the diagram becomes even more dynamic when the arrows of the cycle are flipped to demonstrate the Cycle of Works, humanity's auto-pilot function. Beginning with Achievement, you strive to accomplish things to build a self-made Significance, or something that makes you unique from everyone else.

This is an attempt to find internal Sustenance, which you hope will lead on to Acceptance, either from people or, more dangerously, God himself.

THINKING BIBLICALLY

Jesus' disciples James and John, aka 'the Sons of Thunder', were trapped in the Cycle of Works. Matthew (20:20–28) tells how they came to Jesus and asked to sit at his right and his left in his Kingdom: to achieve a position of Significance.

Despite Jesus making it clear he was going to Jerusalem to die, James and John seem to have assumed Jesus will come out on top in the end and set up a new earthly kingdom. With this in mind, they seek to get in before the other disciples and ask Jesus for influential positions. They are demonstrating the motivation of seeking Significance in order to gain internal Sustenance, leading to outward Acceptance. (This motivation may have come from their ambitious mother, who is in on the request with them.) Their ignorance, despite nearly three years of walking closely with Jesus, should encourage us that we're not the only ones who get stuck in the Cycle of Works.

Jesus knows that there will be one on his right and one on his left in Jerusalem, but these will be criminals on crosses, not princes on thrones. And he also knows that upon the cross he will 'give his life as a ransom' (Matthew 20:28) for the Acceptance that James and John wrongly think can be found in influential positions. Jesus also knows that if this Acceptance is received and allowed to grow, it will free them from the need for worldly Significance through Achievement. Indeed, they will be able to freely embrace Jesus' upside-down Kingdom where 'whoever wants to become great among you must be your servant, and whoever wants to be first must be your slave' (Matthew 20:26).

HOW DO I APPLY IT?

Your entrapment in the Cycle of Works, or your search for Acceptance through Achievement, will usually finds its source in one of the three deadly Ps:

Performance: believing you can be accepted by what you do. You seek Acceptance by proving that you are worthy through achieving things such as 'impressive' job titles, qualifications or sporting prowess.

Possessions: believing you can be accepted by what you have. You seek Acceptance by getting more and more, whether that be through increasing your bank balance, beauty or comfort.

Popularity: believing you can be accepted by what others think of you. You seek Acceptance by gaining favour with others, through striving to make them happy.

Applying the Cycle of Grace takes a concerted effort by remembering how utterly insignificant your performance, possessions and popularity are to your acceptance from Jesus. You don't need to try to gain your own salvation, because it's already been gained for you. Don't try to work yourself into his grace; just acknowledge your need for it.

"'Come to me, all you who are weary and burdened, and I will give you rest. Take my yoke upon you and learn from me, for I am gentle and humble in heart, and you will find rest for your souls'" (Matthew 11:28–29).

Just as we're instructed before a flight to put on our own oxygen mask before we put one on someone else, so we need to first breathe in his love and grace for ourselves before we seek to serve others with it. The nineteenth-century evangelist George Müller impressed this upon his readers:

> Above all things see to it that your souls are happy in the Lord. Other things may press upon you, the Lord's work may even have urgent claims upon your attention, but I deliberately repeat, it is of supreme and paramount importance that you should seek above all things to have your souls truly happy in God Himself. [1]

Applying this principle encourages you towards seeing yourself as Christ-made rather than self-made.

QUESTIONS FOR REFLECTION

Are you in the Cycle of Grace or the Cycle of Works right now?

What helps you stay in the Cycle of Grace?

Which P is most likely to draw you into the Cycle of Works?

GO FURTHER

Read *The Cycle of Grace: Living in Sacred Balance* by Trevor Hudson.[2]

Holistic Spirituality

THE HEART, HEAD, HANDS
AND HUDDLE TRIANGLE
CHRIS

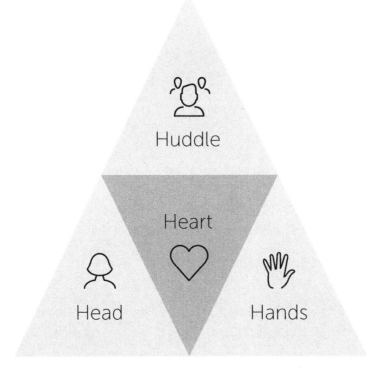

SETTING THE SCENE

'The Combination Person' is a fun drawing game we used to love playing as kids. The first player starts by drawing a head and neck; they fold the paper over and the second player draws a torso and makes another fold. Then the third draws some legs and folds, before the fourth draws a pair of feet. The paper is then unfolded to reveal the combination. The result – a person with a distorted design and shape – often elicits much laughter. To this day, I can still remember the thin, but oversized, butler-cum-surfer we once created!

Sadly, this disjointed picture can also be reflective of our spirituality. Jesus wants to be loved with 'all your heart and with all your soul and with all your mind' (Matthew 22:37). And we are encouraged to work out this relationship with God in a Christian community (Hebrews 10:24–25). But we often emphasise one or another of these elements at the expense of others. The result is an odd combination of spirituality, that if unfolded, would likely make us balk.

WHAT'S THE BIG IDEA?

A single triangle contains four identical triangles that together represent essential building blocks for a holistic, or healthily integrated, Christian spirituality. These are:

Heart. The Heart represents a core connection with Christ, a deep knowing of him. It's related to your emotions but goes even deeper than that, into your will. It's expressed through activities such as personal worship, Scripture meditation, prayer, retreats, counselling, spiritual direction, silence, solitude and reflection. This is the central triangle, demonstrating that all the other triangles flow out from this. It's also the only inward-pointing triangle, primarily representing the inner life.

Hands. This represents the use of your body in service to Jesus. It's expressed through what may naturally come to mind when we think about being the hands and feet of Jesus. It's doing what Jesus did: caring for the sick, embracing the poor and grieving, feeding the hungry and healing the broken.

Head. In reading this book, you're actively practising the Head of spirituality as you're engaging your brain in an attempt to become a more mature disciple of Jesus Christ. Anything that helps strengthen your understanding of God comes into play here. Examples would be personal study through things like books, talks and pilgrimages, which centre on topics such as Scripture, doctrine and church history.

Together the Heart, Hands and Head represent the foundation of and flow into the …

Huddle. This is about coming together with other followers of Jesus. It represents a closeness of community life with other disciples. It will include activities such as communal meals, breaking of bread and wine, prayer, teaching and worship. As the top triangle, it demonstrates how an individual's Heart, Head and Hands act as a gift, in service to the communal Huddle.

The holistic idea is that the four triangles are interdependent, and only through their combined strength does the structure stand firm. If one triangle is removed, or is disproportionately sized, the structure's stability is compromised. The complete triangle together points outward, towards mission, and upward, towards glorifying God.

THINKING BIBLICALLY

Like the Pharisees, we often practise some commands but neglect others: "'Woe to you, teachers of the law and Pharisees, you hypocrites! You give a tenth of your spices – mint, dill and cumin. But you have neglected the more important matters of the law – justice, mercy and faithfulness. You should have practised the latter, without neglecting the former'" (Matthew 23:23). When it comes to the four Hs, there's a biblical emphasis on practising all four:

Heart. Jesus didn't die just to get you into heaven one day but to get heaven into you *today*; he wants to be known in your heart. In Jesus' high priestly prayer in John 17, like a forceful footnote, he explains what it is to have eternal life: "'Now this is eternal life: that they know you, the only true God, and Jesus Christ, whom you have sent'" (John 17:3). This type of knowing is intimate. The same word is used to describe how Mary didn't 'know' Joseph before she gave birth (Matthew 1:25), revealing that they had not been intimate as husband and wife.

It follows then that Jesus wants us to love him with all our hearts (Matthew 22:37), having our hearts undefiled (Matthew 15:18) and soft towards him (Mark 8:17). Therefore, we follow Jesus from our hearts (Romans 6:17, Ephesians 6:6), and we may find them burning within us (Luke 24:32), as we connect with him from there (Ephesians 5:19).

Hands. It was probably the sixteenth-century reformer Martin Luther who said, 'We are saved by faith alone, but that faith is never alone.' It's a great summary of James 2:14–26, which argues that a true and alive faith in Jesus will result in good works, or, in the diagram's terms: Heart will lead to Hands. Indeed, James makes the argument, 'Religion that God our Father accepts as pure and faultless is this: to look after orphans and widows in their distress and to keep oneself from being polluted by the world' (James 1:27). Pragmatically, this means using our bodies, aka Hands, to do godly things and not do ungodly things.

Head. Romans 12:2 says, 'Do not conform to the pattern of this world, but be transformed by the renewing of your mind.' We're encouraged to do this through growing in our knowledge of Jesus (2 Peter 3:18) by letting the Word of God dwell in us richly (Colossians 3:16).

Huddle. There are fifty-seven 'one another' commands in the New Testament, such as loving one another (John 13:34), bearing with one another (Ephesians 4:2 ESV) and not lying to one another (Colossians 3:9). It's impossible to obey these in a silo, so we're also commanded to not give up meeting together (Hebrews 10:25). Indeed, Acts 2:42–47 paints an aspirational picture of a thoroughly committed and unified Huddle.

HOW DO I APPLY IT?

To grow in knowing, understanding and obeying Jesus in a Christian community, this three-phased circular process should help.

Review: Have a think about how you're doing at each H triangle. Ask those close to you how they think you are at each one. Try taking a week to log your practices under the four H triangles.

While it's perfectly normal to have one or two triangles stronger than the others, you've hopefully discovered some room for growth in the weaker ones. Perhaps one triangle doesn't even exist for you, and like a three-wheeled car, you're moving forward but not effectively.

Learn: Explore how you can grow the H you want to work on. The Knowing God: Divine Connections diagram on the following page will help with that. Ask others for their insights. Create a plan.

Practise: Put the plan into action, and then review again.

QUESTIONS FOR REFLECTION

Draw four triangles proportionate to the size of how you think you are doing at each one. What stands out to you?

What weekly practice could enlarge your smallest triangle?

Who do you know who excels in each of the four Hs? Why do they excel in them?

GO FURTHER

To take a survey on your Heart, Head and Hands strengths check out wearemakingdisciples.com. (N.B. The Huddle is not distinct in this test but is incorporated into the other Hs.)

Knowing God

DIVINE CONNECTIONS
ANDY

SETTING THE SCENE

Over the course of my life, I have been to a lot of Christian conferences and heard a lot of inspiring talks. I remember hearing one speaker share about how he spends every morning in two hours of prayer and how powerfully he connects with God. For a while I set my alarm for 5 a.m. and tried to do the same.

At another conference, there was a renowned biblical scholar sharing how she read through large swathes of the Bible every day, soaking herself in God's Word. Her talk was contagious, and I wanted to do the same, so I tried to carve out chunks of my day to dive into Scripture on a whole new level.

And then at another conference, a speaker shared about how he lives in a deprived area and spends time with those that everyone else ignores – the homeless, the destitute, the drug addicts. He shared how he encountered God tangibly as he got alongside the most vulnerable. I was blown away by his stories and tried to befriend anyone who looked remotely marginalised.

I am not sure if you have ever done the same, but when we hear or meet inspirational people of faith, we can try to find a secret formula that will take us deeper in our relationship with God. We can think that engaging with God is somehow formulaic and that a real encounter only looks like what we have heard shared from a platform.

WHAT'S THE BIG IDEA?

We all relate to God differently.

There is no one-size-fits-all when it comes to our relationship with God. In fact, it can become dangerous when we try to copy other people's walks with God or try to make others copy what works for us. Gary Thomas, author of *Sacred Pathways*, writes, 'Thou shalt not covet thy neighbor's spiritual walk. After all, it's his, not yours. Better to discover the path God designed for you to take, a path marked by growth and fulfillment, based on your unique spiritual temperament.'[3]

Gary's book explores nine common approaches to loving God that have been outlined in the diagram above. Very often we will prefer a combination of a few of these temperaments, and as we journey in our faith, our preferences may also change over time.

THINKING BIBLICALLY

In the Psalms we see a spectrum of ways for engaging with God in the highs and lows of life. Psalm 100 is specifically a psalm of thanks. The psalmist teaches us both why to give thanks and how to give thanks, and in five verses he touches on some of the different ways we engage with God.

In verses 1–2 and 4, he calls us to use our mouths. He encourages us to shout for joy, to make a joyful (not necessarily pleasant!) noise and to sing songs. And yet the first part of verse 2, 'Worship the LORD with gladness', implies not just sung worship but service. *Barnes' Notes on the Whole Bible* says that this can be interpreted as 'Serve the LORD with gladness.'[4] So there is the call to give thanks to God with acts of service and the things we do. And it's clear that the psalmist wants us to serve with the right attitude – gladness – too!

And then, in verse 3, there is the phrase 'Know that the LORD is God.' This verse contains the idea of knowing God with our minds. We are to connect with him using our intellect because he wants to be known. And in verse 4, the concept of entering his courts carries the idea that we should be connecting with God in our worship corporately too. Our faith is not just something we do as individuals but as a body of people.

As we read through Scripture, we see there are a multitude of ways in which we can engage with God.

HOW DO I APPLY IT?

Scan through the list of the nine pathways. Which ones are you most drawn to?

NATURALISTS: LOVING GOD OUTDOORS
Just as Jesus often sought solace in nature as a place to pray and be refilled, so Naturalists connect with God in the power, the complexity and the beauty of creation. They humble themselves as they remember God is Creator. 'For since the creation of the world God's invisible qualities … have been clearly seen, being understood from what has been made' (Romans 1:20).

SENSATES: LOVING GOD WITH THE SENSES
Using taste, touch, smell, sound and sight, Sensates draw upon the likes of the Old Testament prophets and John's book of Revelation. They connect with God powerfully through the arts.

TRADITIONALISTS: LOVING GOD THROUGH RITUAL AND SYMBOL
Many of our religious rituals embody spiritual truths. Traditionalists journey with God as they celebrate religious festivals and rhythms.

ASCETICS: LOVING GOD IN SOLITUDE AND SIMPLICITY
Monastic in heritage, Ascetics draw upon the disciplines of solitude and simplicity. They choose to deny themselves the possibility of being distracted by their senses.

ACTIVISTS: LOVING GOD THROUGH CONFRONTATION

Activists are people who relate to God best when they are confronting injustice and taking a stand for what is right. They may be passionate evangelists and social reformers.

CAREGIVERS: LOVING GOD BY LOVING OTHERS

Visiting the elderly, nursing the sick and caring for the homeless may be just some of the ways Caregivers journey with God.

ENTHUSIASTS: LOVING GOD WITH MYSTERY AND CELEBRATION

Enthusiasts often have a joyous and celebratory style of worship. They experience God in the buzz and the awe and often have a high expectancy to see the supernatural.

CONTEMPLATIVES: LOVING GOD THROUGH ADORATION

The Contemplative first and foremost wants to adore God. They practise the presence of God using things like the Jesus Prayer: 'Lord Jesus Christ, Son of God, have mercy on me, a sinner.'

INTELLECTUALS: LOVING GOD WITH THE MIND

Intellectuals best relate to God when they study the Bible, doctrines, theology and church history. They connect most with God when learning, and it's only after intellectual revelation that they respond in adoration.

We will all be attracted to different pathways – this may be influenced by our personality, our upbringing or our faith experiences. We may also change our preferences in different seasons of our lives, laying aside certain pathways at certain times and taking up new ones.

Each of the nine pathways also has pitfalls. It's important to be aware of these. For example, Naturalists can begin to idolise nature, and Traditionalists can lose the meaning behind the rituals.

The pathways give us an opportunity to understand more of how we relate to God, but they also reveal new ways in which we might explore how we express our love for God. As you scan the list, are there any pathways you haven't experienced that you would like to try?

QUESTIONS FOR REFLECTION

What do the practices of your preferred pathways look like?

What are some of the pitfalls linked to these ways of engaging with God?

How do the pathways help us to help others in their walk with God?

GO FURTHER

Read *Sacred Pathways* by Gary Thomas.

Strategic Praying

THE HANDY PRAYER TOOL

CHRIS

Family & Friends

Teachers & Leaders in Your Life

People in Authority

The Weak

You

SETTING THE SCENE

On 23 May 1940, during World War II, King George VI called the United Kingdom to a national day of prayer in response to a potentially devastating loss of British troops. Christians came out to pray in their thousands, and amazing things began to happen:

- The chasing Nazi army were confoundingly ordered to halt by Hitler.
- Bad weather grounded much of the Luftwaffe and kept the skies relatively clear from bombardment.
- The sea surrounding Dunkirk became extraordinarily calm, providing safe passage.

This resulted in over 338,000 troops being rescued from Dunkirk, far more than expected. Such was the significance of the rescue that a national day of thanksgiving was held just a few days later, to thank God for answered prayer.

Stories like this remind us of the power of prayer, and invite us to use our prayers for greater concerns, such as peace and a proclamation of the gospel, rather than just the small and immediate personal struggles of life.

WHAT'S THE BIG IDEA?

Knowing what to pray for is often a prayer request in itself! But one helpful tool you'll likely have at your disposal is your hands. While this diagram may appear a little childish, it's a helpful visual to discipline you towards more strategic praying. So, hold up your hands in front of you now, place them together and put your thumbs close to your heart – and you're ready to pray …

First, use your thumb. As the thumb is closest to your physical heart, start by praying for those closest to your emotional heart: your family and friends. Pray they would be drawn close to the Father's heart and for anything else on your mind for them.

Second, use your index finger. This is the one you usually point with, so use it as a prompt to pray for the teachers and leaders in your life, those who direct you: your local church leaders, your small group leaders, anyone training or mentoring you in any capacity now. Pray that they would give you wise counsel and that you would appropriately submit to their godly authority.

Third, use your middle finger. This is the finger that stands out above the others, so use it as a reminder to pray for 'kings and all those in authority, that we may live peaceful and quiet lives in all godliness and holiness' (1 Timothy 2:2). Thank God and pray for local, national and global leaders.

Fourth, use your ring finger. This is your weakest finger, so let it remind you to pray for the weak. Pray for those you personally know who are struggling at this time and for those in your local town and city who are abandoned or abused.

Fifth, use your little finger or pinky. This is your last finger, and now you have looked not only to your own interests but to the interests of others (see Philippians 2:4), you're ready to bring your own personal requests before God, hopefully now with a less self-centred perspective.

THINKING BIBLICALLY

It's funny how in church we're asked to close our eyes and bow our heads to pray, when Jesus seemed to pray with his eyes wide open and pointed up to heaven (Mark 7:34, John 11:41, John 17:1). While it may seem pernickety, what we do with our bodies when we pray can help or hinder the process. The Handy Prayer Tool is one way to engage your body as you pray. It also imitates Jesus who 'lifted up his hands' in prayer (Luke 24:50), which is in line with Paul's instruction to us: 'I want the men everywhere to pray, lifting up holy hands without anger or disputing' (1 Timothy 2:8).

HOW DO I APPLY IT?

According to church history, James, the once earthly brother of Jesus, went on to acquire the nickname 'Old Camel Knees', because of the amount of time he spent praying on his knees. As a leader, you are called to lead from your knees; your prayer life is intrinsically linked to your leadership life.

It was the evangelist Smith Wigglesworth who said, 'I don't often spend more than half an hour in prayer at one time, but I never go more than half an hour without praying.'[5] Whenever you find yourself with a five-minute window, if you commit this diagram to memory, you will have five key themes to pray about throughout your day. Many leaders find it helpful to keep a journal as a reminder of whom and what to pray for, but, unlike a book, this handy tool goes wherever you go. You may like to think about using it at set times, such as before or after meals, on your commute, or even when you use the bathroom!

If you have a little more time, you may find the following longer Handy Prayer outline helpful:

1. Start by lifting both your hands stretched to heaven, and bless, worship and adore Jesus.
2. Move on to the Handy Prayer outline above.
3. Finish by opening your hands to heaven by your side, becoming aware of the presence of God and waiting silently to hear his voice.

QUESTIONS FOR REFLECTION

How would you rate your personal prayer life out of ten? What would it take to improve that score by one or two points?

How do you find praying for yourself last? Why do you think that is?

GO FURTHER

Check out the Prayer Course from 24-7 Prayer: prayercourse.org.

Watch author and pastor Rick Warren talking about prayer: saddleback.com/watch/40-days-of-prayer/how-to-pray-throughout-your-day.

Performing Well

THE EMOTIONAL ENERGY MATRIX
ANDY

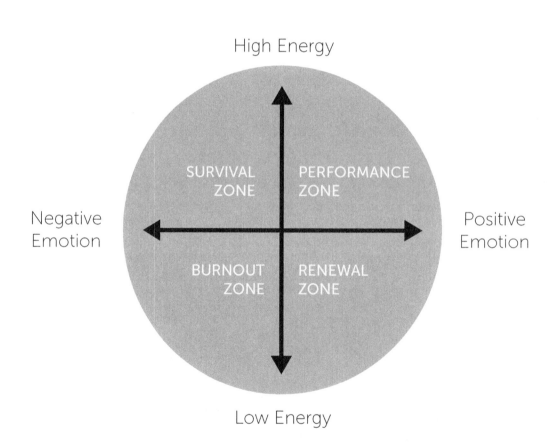

SETTING THE SCENE

Over the years I have done a good number of endurance races, ranging from an Iron Man to a 10km Loch Lomond swim, the toughest of which was the Jurassic Coast 100 ultramarathon. This involved 105 miles (five more than I was expecting) non-stop running and walking along a coastline with 15,000 feet of elevation.

It was tough. There was the heat, the ascents, the chafing (the Vaseline and special breathable underwear that worked for fifty miles didn't work for 105), the headlands that looked closer than they were and the lack of sleep. In total, I was on my feet for thirty-four hours and thirty-four minutes. By the end I was exhausted, and I looked so haggard that dog walkers and local residents kept asking me if I was okay.

On the one hand, how well you do in these kinds of events is down to physical training, grit and determination, but a vital component is understanding what your body needs. In my training, I quickly learnt the importance of electrolyte tablets and water consumption to replace all the lost salt from sweat, as well as the need for the right solids that could be kept down and processed efficiently into energy.

Those who regularly run ultramarathons understand their bodies so well. They know how much fluid and how many calories they need for a set distance. But often in our everyday life, when we're just going through the motions, we can be pretty bad at knowing what our bodies need and how to fulfil those needs.

WHAT'S THE BIG IDEA?

Tony Schwartz is founder and president of The Energy Project, which aims to help people achieve more in less time. In his book *The Way We're Working Isn't Working*,[6] he argues that in the modern workplace, we often think of ourselves as machines who can keep outputting in a flat, linear fashion for long stints of time. But because we're not computers, this is not working for us. He notes:

> *The way we're working isn't working for us, for our employers, or for our families. It's not the number of hours we work that determines how much value we create. Rather it's the quantity and quality of energy we bring to whatever hours we work.*[7]

THE FOUR ZONES EXPLAINED

Schwartz's Emotional Energy Matrix has four zones, which helps us become more aware of our energy and emotion. Although all of us will have experienced each of the four zones, the aim is to spend as much time as possible on the right-hand side of the diagram, switching between the Performance and Renewal zones. We find ourselves on the left-hand side of the diagram when we strive to stay in the Performance Zone and haven't made time or space for recovery.

Survival Zone: Negative Emotion and High Energy
Many of us can still perform well in this zone, but we can

be feeling angry, fearful or stressed. Although energy is high, it can be driven by high negative emotions, as we try to meet multiple demands. This zone becomes an issue as it can lead you to the Burnout Zone, so it's important you make time to recharge. For example, exercise can be a helpful outlet for high energy levels fuelled by stress or other negative emotions.

Burnout Zone: Negative Emotion and Low Energy
When we're in this zone, things can feel hopeless. We are exhausted and fed up. If you're in a leadership role, you may appear to your team as apathetic and cynical. To avoid this zone and to move out of it, it's important to make space to recharge.

Renewal Zone: Positive Emotion and Low Energy
This zone can appear to be a luxury, but recovery is essential if you want to perform well. However, it's not helpful to permanently stay in this zone, as eventually we begin to coast and simply do the bare minimum. Although we may be getting the job done, we are not working to our potential. To avoid getting stuck in this zone, we need a sense of urgency. When we are rejuvenated, clearly defined goals with timelines often help us and our teams move towards the Performance Zone.

Performance Zone: Positive Emotion and High Energy
This is where we thrive. In this zone we are highly motivated to achieve, and our teams follow suit. In this zone, we are passionate, well connected with others and effective. This zone is not without challenge, but we have the right energy and emotional state to tackle it. While we are in this zone, we need to be aware of our energy levels and emotions to make sure that we can take the necessary action to stop us from moving into the Survival or Burnout zones.

THINKING BIBLICALLY

Elijah was not in the Performance Zone when he was in the wilderness in 1 Kings 19. Terrified for his life, he fled into the middle of nowhere and said to God, 'I have had enough LORD… Take my life, I am no better than my ancestors' (1 Kings 19:4).

He was a broken man.

And yet, by the end of the chapter, he has been re-commissioned and is back serving God. Mapping his experience onto the diagram above, we see he goes through a Renewal Zone. He sleeps and rests. He eats. He drinks and rehydrates. He sleeps again. Then he eats and drinks again.

Interestingly, before he converses with Elijah, God meets his very real physical needs so that he is able to re-commission him and to find a successor.

HOW DO I APPLY IT?

To deal with our energy levels and emotions, we need to be aware of our physical, emotional, mental and spiritual needs. We all need to create rhythms in our lives that give us renewal time, whether that's enough sleep or spending quality time with loved ones.

But there are also things we can do in the everyday flow of work to help us stay in the right-hand quadrants.

Physically, are we taking regular breaks in our working day? Are we making space for exercise? Are we making sure we don't skip meals?

Emotionally, do we spend time each day doing something that we enjoy, that gives us energy and is life-giving? Do we make space for the relationships that are important to us? Do we encourage colleagues and celebrate wins?

Mentally, do we recognise that there are both external and internal distractions? Do we have the right external environment that allows us to focus on work without incessant interruptions? To avoid internal dialogue distractions, do we make space to sit quietly and figure things out?

Spiritually, how does what we do connect with our God-given purpose? Where can we appropriately take moments to reflect on God's call upon our lives?

None of us can live in the right-hand quadrants all the time. Life is often messy, but this diagram helps you consider – both for yourself and your team – how you can move towards working in a more optimal zone.

QUESTIONS FOR REFLECTION

Which zone do you spend most of your time in?

What physical, emotional, mental and spiritual disciplines give you energy and allow you to perform well?

Where is your team spending most of their time? If you are in a different zone to your team, what can you do about it?

GO FURTHER

Read *The Way We're Working Isn't Working* by Tony Schwartz.

Getting to Know Yourself

THE JOHARI WINDOW

CHRIS

	KNOWN TO SELF	NOT KNOWN TO SELF
KNOWN TO OTHERS	Arena	Blind Spot
NOT KNOWN TO OTHERS	Facade	Unknown

SETTING THE SCENE

When paintballing with some friends before my wedding, I thought the pink tutu I was forced to wear on top of my overalls was attracting more attention than it deserved. Only towards the end of the day was it pointed out to me that my so-called 'friends' had also slapped a large, luminous yellow 'X' on my back without my knowing, and that everyone at the paintball park had been instructed to shoot the guy with said 'X' on his back. Needless to say, once I discovered this, the offending target was immediately removed.

When something previously unknown becomes known to us, it gives us an opportunity to take appropriate action. The Johari Window gives language and provides pathways for that process.

WHAT'S THE BIG IDEA?

When it comes to self-awareness, knowledge is crucial. This quadrant, developed by Christians Joseph Luft and Harrington Ingham, [8] hence the name Johari, categorises knowledge into four quadrants.

ARENA

In this quadrant are the details about you that both you and others know. This covers everything from the basics, such as your physical characteristics, to the quirks, such as your persistent lateness or your funny laugh.

FACADE

In this category are the things you know about yourself but others don't. These range from your secret loves, such as cheesy pop music, to the more serious struggles and sins we all seek to hide.

BLIND SPOT

In this quadrant are the things that other people know about you that you don't know about. For example, you may not be aware that you intimidate others, but those around you are very aware of it.

UNKNOWN

In the final category lies the knowledge about you that neither you nor others are aware of, for example, a trauma from your childhood that has had an unknown but profound effect on your life.

THINKING BIBLICALLY

In Luke 6, Jesus uses the hyperbolic idea of someone trying to remove a speck of sawdust from someone's eye when there's a whole plank of wood in their own. Jesus knows that we're often quick to spot room for improvement in others but often fall short at seeing things in our own lives. He therefore calls us to 'first take the plank out of your eye, and then you will see clearly to remove the speck from your brother's eye' (Luke 6:42).

If removing a piece of sawdust from an eye is a painful process, removing a plank would be far worse. But if we are going to lead others, then we need to heed the advice in Romans to 'not think of yourself more highly than you ought' (12:3). Otherwise, we will be like the blind leading the blind (Matthew 15:14).

It's important to be aware that those living primarily in the Facade category receive some of Jesus' most critical words, most starkly in Matthew 23:27–28:

> *'Woe to you, teachers of the law and Pharisees, you hypocrites! You are like whitewashed tombs, which look beautiful on the outside but on the inside are full of the bones of the dead and everything unclean. In the same way, on the outside you appear to people as righteous but on the inside you are full of hypocrisy and wickedness.'*

HOW DO I APPLY IT?

Each of the four categories has a unique application.

ARENA

I wonder if you've ever had a lift from someone in a car that's full of old rubbish? Both you and the driver know that the smell emanating from the rubbish is staying with you for as long as that car journey takes. But just because that knowledge exists doesn't mean it has to stay that way. The driver could pull over and put the rubbish in the nearest bin.

In the same way, we often seek to normalise undesired behaviours we have that others are familiar with. We say things like, 'That's just me; everybody knows it!' But just because we're aware of issues doesn't mean a clean-up operation isn't needed.

FACADE

There is an integrity gap in us all, as we hide or play-act in order to appear better than we are. Closing that gap is a lifelong process that comes about by vulnerably and courageously sharing those things we know about ourselves that we seek to conceal. Obviously, this is a delicate process of finding the right people to share the right things with at the right time, and there is always risk involved as we trust others, but as we do, we become more authentic leaders.

BLIND SPOT

There's a story about a child who adopted a cat on holiday. He fed it, stroked it, watered it … loved it. In fact, he loved it so much over that two-week holiday that he smuggled it back home to live with the cat he already owned. However, tragedy struck, when, the morning after he returned, the child went downstairs to find his new beloved cat had killed the cat he already had. The murdering cat was taken to the vet at once, where it was revealed to the child that the cat he had adopted and smuggled was not actually a cat but a giant rat!

Perhaps our blind spots aren't quite so exaggerated, but, by definition, they are those things that we cannot see. We therefore need knowledgeable friends, like the vet in the story, to help us see what we cannot.

Most leaders think they have an open-door policy, where people can speak to them when they want, but as leaders it's important we actively and humbly invite feedback into our lives. This will help us move items that were once in the Blind Spot category into the Arena category.

UNKNOWN

It's important to be aware of, but not intimated by, this category. Simply acknowledging there are issues that you and others can't see at the moment opens us up to a journey of discovery with God as he highlights the issues he wants to raise in our life.

QUESTIONS FOR REFLECTION

What Arena issues have you grown content with?

What Facade issues do you have that you would like to move into the Arena? How will you do this?

Who could you ask about Blind Spots in your life?

How could you start to explore the Unknown category?

GO FURTHER

Read *Of Human Interaction: Johari Model* by Joseph Luft. Various organisations can help you to conduct a 360-Degree Peer Review, which gives you an opportunity to discover Blind Spots at your work.[9]

Going Deeper

THE ICEBERG OF EMOTIONAL HEALTH

ANDY

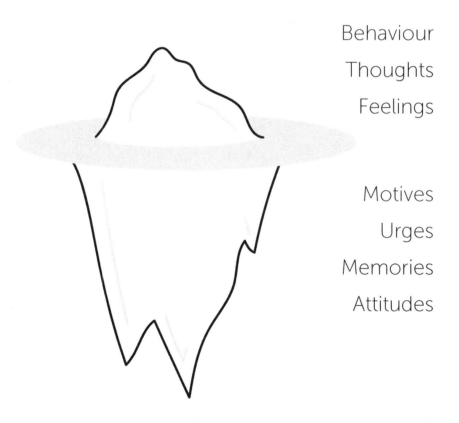

Behaviour

Thoughts

Feelings

Motives

Urges

Memories

Attitudes

SETTING THE SCENE

On 14 April 1912 Frederick Fleet and Reginald Lee were occupying the crow's nest of a large cruiser ship, twenty-nine metres above the deck. The crew, aware of ice in the vicinity, did not reduce the ship's speed, and continued to steam ahead at 25mph.

At 11.39 p.m., Fleet spotted an iceberg in *Titanic's* path. He rang the lookout bell three times and telephoned the bridge to inform Officer James Moody. Fleet asked, 'Is there anyone there?' Moody replied, 'Yes, what do you see?' Fleet replied, 'Iceberg, right ahead!'

Quartermaster Robert Hichens then changed the ship's course. But it was too late …

An underwater spur of ice scraped along the starboard side of the ship for about seven seconds. About five minutes after the collision, all of *Titanic's* engines had stopped, leaving the bow of the ship facing north and slowly drifting south, with damage extended over a length of about 300 feet.

The ship began to flood immediately, with water pouring in at an estimated rate of seven long tons (7.1t) per second, fifteen times faster than it could be pumped out. The ship eventually disappeared from view at 2.20 a.m.

There is much more to an iceberg than what is visible on the surface, much like our lives. The top 10 per cent above the waterline represents the seen and known parts of us: the things we do, say, think and feel. Sometimes we can kid ourselves that this is all we are.

WHAT'S THE BIG IDEA?

The adage 'tip of the iceberg' reminds us that there is a lot more under the surface than we can see. Peter Scazzero, founder of Emotionally Healthy Discipleship, helpfully takes this idea to address our emotions, recognising that how we handle our emotions will impact our relationship with God, with others and with ourselves.

When it comes to exploring our emotions, we can often either over complicate things, believing we all need emergency specialist help, or oversimplify things, thinking we just need to change what we see above the surface – most specifically, what we do. Too often we are only bothered with changing what other people see rather than doing some deeper reflection on what is beneath the surface.

Being disciples of Jesus means we spend time reflecting on the truths of Scripture and inviting God's Spirit to transform us, but we also need to look into our hearts to become more aware of our Motives, Urges, Memories and Attitudes.

THINKING BIBLICALLY

"'The wall of Jerusalem is broken down, and its gates have been burned with fire'" (Nehemiah 1:3).

As soon as Nehemiah hears this report from his brother, he is overcome with emotion. For Nehemiah, the walls of Jerusalem were significant. They were tied to the promises of God, and an unwalled city was a disgrace. It was shameful.

He sits – an act of humility – and he weeps. He allows himself to connect with his emotions.

He then turns to mourning, fasting and praying. In essence, he is acknowledging the issues that have caused this reaction, and in the prayer that follows (verses 5–11), we see how he processes what to do next. In this brilliant prayer he:

- celebrates God's character;
- reminds us that we can get God's attention;
- remembers the promises of God;
- acknowledges God's power; and
- prays for specific practicalities.

The emotion and the weeping above the surface were prayerfully processed so that he understood the underlying issues and could ascertain what to do next.

HOW DO I APPLY IT?

When we fail to reflect on what is beneath the surface of our lives, we can often lack self-awareness, afraid of being vulnerable and suppressing our emotions. Our emotions are a God-given gift to help us process the world around us. If we are to become effective leaders, we need to ensure we adopt healthy practices to ensure our emotional wellbeing.

First, we need to stop and make space to listen to our emotions, perhaps using the Emotions Wheel diagram which is in the next chapter.

Second, we need to stop and ask why we are feeling these emotions. We need to explore the underlying causes. By acknowledging and naming these realities, we raise our emotional awareness. This in turn enables us to process our emotions in a healthy way.

Third, we need to work out how to process the underlying causes. In part, this involves speaking the truth of Christ into the issue, but it may also require practical actions, such as forgiving someone.

For example, if we have a challenging meeting and leave feeling betrayed, we need to stop and take some time to recognise that emotion. We then need to ask why we are feeling this way. Has a memory been triggered that's exacerbated the situation? We speak God's truth into the situation, and we might ask someone to pray for us. We might also need to offer or ask for forgiveness.

QUESTIONS FOR REFLECTION

Thinking through the last week, are there moments when you have experienced strong emotions?

Have you taken the time to process them?

How might this diagram help?

Jesus spoke to his closest friends about how he was feeling. Who can you share the 'under-the-iceberg' emotions with?

GO FURTHER

Read *The Emotionally Healthy Leader* by Peter Scazzero.[10]

Feel the Feelings

THE EMOTIONS WHEEL
CHRIS

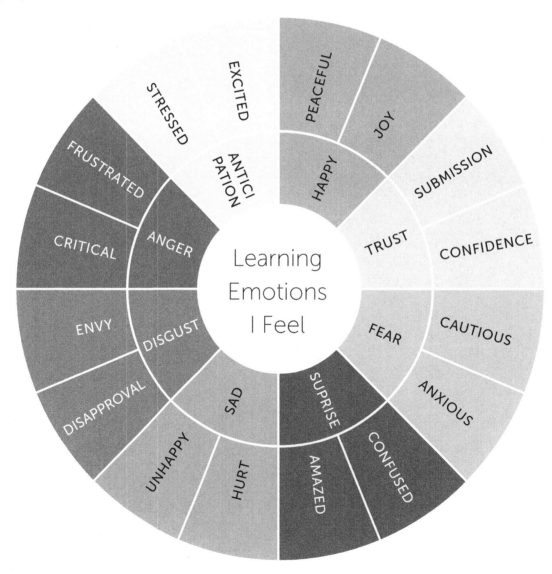

SETTING THE SCENE

In 2008, I sat in my crowded office, thinking I was feeling sick. I had just finished taking notes for a story from a phone call with a bereaved mother, when a wave of what I thought was nausea rumbled in my stomach. She had intricately detailed the events surrounding the sudden death of her only son and went on to slowly unpack her agony of grief. Phone down, I ran to the toilet and locked the cubicle door, my whole body trembling. But to my surprise what came out was not vomit but emotion. I let out a large wail from the pit of my stomach, followed by at least ten minutes of uncontrollable crying.

Just a few months earlier I had stood by my father's bedside and watched him slip from this life into the next. It was as if hearing the mother's grief over the phone had finally broken through a thin lid that was suppressing all the grief I was containing over the loss of my father.

I look back on that moment with empathy; I was emotionally juvenile, having little understanding as to how I was feeling at any given time. If I looked sad, and anyone asked how I was, I was always 'just tired'. The shock of that event started me on a journey towards becoming more emotionally aware, and the Emotions Wheel diagram has played a significant part in that process.

Leaders often have an innate ability to ignore current emotional states to work towards a bigger goal. But ignoring your emotions long-term is dangerous. Why? Because those suppressed emotions will somehow and somewhere rear their heads, usually in ugly ways. They won't relent until they are noticed.

WHAT'S THE BIG IDEA?

You can have all the IQ (Intelligence Quotient) in the world, but if your EQ (Emotional Quotient) is weak, your ability to function well as a leader will always be stunted. I'm sure you can think of a leader who has an unbalanced mix of IQ to EQ. Related to the Iceberg of Emotional Health diagram (page 40), the Emotions Wheel can help you explore what's going on under the water, behind what others see, and increase your EQ to help you lead more effectively.

The Emotions Wheel above is a reduced version of Robert Plutchik's Emotions Wheel.[11] Using it can be broken down into three simple steps.

1. RECOGNISE

Start in the middle of the circle and slowly work round the list of eight emotions, until one of them stands out more than the others as to how you may be feeling in that moment. The eight words may not completely resonate with you right now, or several may pop out, but if you had to choose just one, what would it be? The aim here is to take a first broad step on an emotional awareness journey.

2. CONFIRM

Once you have selected one of the eight emotions, you can seek to confirm this feeling by looking at the opposite emotion on the wheel. For example, if you chose 'trust', the opposite would be 'disgust'. Does this opposite emotion confirm that the first emotion you selected is roughly how you may be feeling? If not, you could go back to step one. If it is, continue to step three.

3. EXPLORE

Now look at the two words that stem from the first word you selected. For example, 'angry' would be 'frustrated' and 'critical'. Spend a few moments thinking about which word is the best fit for your emotional state right now. Try saying it out loud. For example, 'Right now, I'm feeling peaceful.' Does it resonate? Then explore further by asking why you think you may be feeling this way.

THINKING BIBLICALLY

We see emotional awareness expressed throughout Scripture, but most vividly in the Psalms where authors express distress (Psalm 4:1), peace (Psalm 4:8), lament (Psalm 5:1), anguish (Psalm 6:3), sorrow (Psalm 13:2), gladness (Psalm 16:9), trust (Psalm 25:2), loneliness (Psalm 25:16), confidence (Psalm 27:13) and joy (Psalm 30:11), among many others.

We also see characters throughout the Bible express incredibly challenging feelings:

- **Job**: 'Why did I not perish at birth, and die as I came from the womb?' (Job 3:11).
- **Jonah**: 'Now, Lord, take away my life, for it is better for me to die than to live' (Jonah 4:3).
- **David**: 'The king was shaken. He went up to the room over the gateway and wept. As he went, he said: "O my son Absalom! My son, my son Absalom! If only I had died instead of you – O Absalom, my son, my son!"' (2 Samuel 18:33).
- **Jeremiah**: 'Cursed be the day I was born! … Why did I ever come out of the womb to see trouble and sorrow and to end my days in shame?' (Jeremiah 20:14,18).

- **Peter**: 'And he went outside and wept bitterly' (Luke 22:62).
- **Paul**: 'We were under great pressure, far beyond our ability to endure, so that we despaired of life itself. Indeed, we felt we had received the sentence of death' (2 Corinthians 1:8–9).
- **Jesus**: '"My soul is overwhelmed with sorrow to the point of death"' (Mark 14:34).

Knowing this biblical freedom to discover and express our feelings is so helpful, no matter how 'negative' we may think our emotions are. Indeed Charles Spurgeon, a great Christian leader of the nineteenth century, felt secure to express, 'I am the subject of depression so fearful that I hope none of you ever get to such extremes of wretchedness as I go to.'[12]

HOW DO I APPLY IT?

Carrying a copy of the Wheel with you, perhaps as an image on your phone, and doing the check-in process a few times throughout your day, will enhance your ability to know how you're feeling at any given moment.

Using the Wheel is the emotional equivalent of lifting weights in the gym; it strengthens an awareness of our feelings. So it's common for a basic exercise like this to initially feel quite strenuous, especially for the emotionally unaware.

This strengthened EQ will bring many benefits, such as:

- helping to provide emotional stamina. For example, you feel peaceful after some personal space, so recognise your need for more in order to be at your best.

- raising red flags for when you need to take action. For example, you feel guilty and so ask for forgiveness for upsetting someone.
- improving communication. For example, you recognise you have been worrying about a decision you have made, so you share that feeling with someone the decision will impact, to gain their perspective.
- deepening your prayer life. For example, you feel a surge of joy following a talk with a friend, so express a new depth of gratitude to God in that moment.

It's also helpful to be aware how our emotional world changes through our life. For example, pastor and author Gordon MacDonald proposes we have a tendency to ask the following unique questions in different decades of our lives:

Teens – Who am I and who am I becoming?

20s – What am I going to do with my life and with whom?

30s – Now that I have all these responsibilities and obligations, how do I manage all these priorities?

40s – Am I a success or a failure?

50s – As I move into the second half of life, who is this younger generation that wants me out of the way and how do I cope with the disappointments in my life?

60s – How much longer can I do what defines me or do I change?

70s – How do I live with loss?

80s – Does anyone remember who I once was? Can anyone remember?

Final Question – What happens when I die?[13]

These can help you recognise that the daily feelings you're having may relate to a broader phase of life's emotions.

QUESTIONS FOR REFLECTION

How much do you think about the value of EQ in daily life?

How can you become more aware of your EQ?

How are you feeling right now? Use the Emotions Wheel to check in with yourself.

GO FURTHER

Use Ignatius Loyola's 'Examen' prayer at the end of your day. This will help you think through your day and shed light on your emotional journey throughout it: ignatianspirituality.com/ignatian-prayer/the-examen.

Watch 'Leadership Advice For Every Decade of Your Life with Gordon MacDonald': youtube.com/watch?v=lmO5OLpFtmc.

Intentional Connectedness

THE SPIRITUAL GROWTH NETWORK

CHRIS

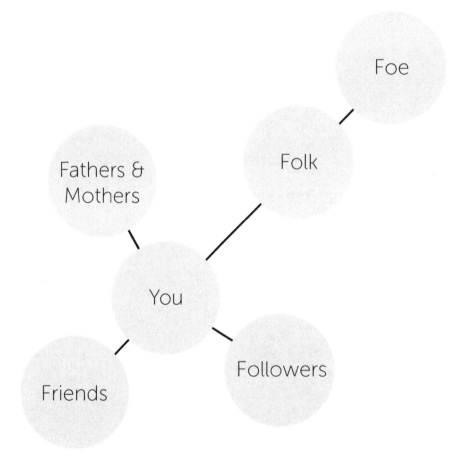

SETTING THE SCENE

In 2003, our dad initiated an email exchange between Andy and me, himself and his dad. We traded stories of how we came to faith, and how we attempted to live out that faith through life's highs and lows. It sparked the publication of a book called *Destiny*,[14] which initiated other multi-generational families of faith to undergo the same process. Communicating across the generations strengthened the faith of all involved, as we each shared our battles and victories.

God designed us to need one another, and generational family structures – although often fragmented and complex – are part of his masterplan. Children raised in a loving family environment are more likely to flourish and become good parents of children, who have a good chance of becoming good parents themselves. In a similar way, for spiritual growth to happen, we need to be surrounded by spiritual family – those who may or may not be part of our biological family but are brothers, sisters, mothers, fathers, sons and daughters in the Lord. Just like our biological family, there will be some relationships where we are learning from others and some where we are helping others to grow in their faith.

WHAT'S THE BIG IDEA?

God can and does use all relationships in our lives. Sometimes the relationships we have with those who aren't Christians can helpfully stretch our faith, but when it comes to thinking about spiritual growth within our Christian family, there are five types of relationships to be aware of.

FATHERS AND MOTHERS

When you're around spiritual parents, it's predominantly you who is growing. These people may not necessarily be ahead of you in years, but they are ahead of you in their maturity in Christ. Often ideas are caught, not just taught; you pick up and positively copy some of their behaviours.

FRIENDS

When you're around Friends, both you and they grow. Friends are those who are there for one another through thick and thin. Our growth and their growth happens in all sorts of ways, but it's often our Friends who lovingly challenge us.

FOLLOWERS

When you're around Followers, you may grow in your faith to some degree, but it's predominantly the Followers who are growing. While it's true that we grow as we go – spiritual growth comes through giving to others – if we are constantly only surrounded by Followers, we'll eventually grow blunt and hinder our Followers.

These three sets of relationships should ideally be closest to you for your spiritual growth, as outlined in the diagram.

If you want to be intentional about your own and others' spiritual growth, you need Fathers and Mothers, Friends and Followers close. The following two relationship sets shouldn't divert your focus.

FOLK

This describes people who just aren't interested in growing in Christ or assisting others in that endeavour. They may be lovely people, but when push comes to shove, they've plateaued.

FOE

Whether consciously or not, this group is actively intent on decreasing your spiritual growth. The old adage 'keep your friends close and your enemies closer' doesn't hold, as spending lots of time with Foes will curtail your growth in the Lord.

THINKING BIBLICALLY

The Bible instructs us to prudently think about our relationships: 'The righteous choose their friends carefully' (Proverbs 12:26), because 'bad company corrupts good character' (1 Corinthians 15:33). We're encouraged to choose close relationships with people who aren't 'hot-tempered' (Proverbs 22:24) or 'unreliable' (Proverbs 18:24), so that we can 'Walk with the wise and become wise' (Proverbs 13:20).

The idea of allowing distance in some relationships to intentionally focus on others may seem ungracious. However, Jesus modelled this when he sent away the rich young ruler, who 'went away sad', unwilling to sell all he had (Matthew 19:22); and with the follower who wanted to bury his father, to whom Jesus said, "'Let the dead bury

their own dead'" (Luke 9:60). It appears Jesus even distanced himself from his own family for a period, to focus on his followers (Matthew 12:46–50).

We can see the relational network of the five Fs in many lives throughout the Bible, but most vividly through Paul's.

FATHERS AND MOTHERS

Barnabas, 'a good man, full of the Holy Spirit and faith' (Acts 11:24), vouched for Paul in Jerusalem, by speaking of his fearless preaching (Acts 9:26–27). Barnabas searched Paul out in Tarsus, to serve alongside him in Antioch (Acts 11:25). No wonder the Holy Spirit commends this relationship (Acts 13:2–4).

FRIENDS

Priscilla and Aquila were able to explain the ways of God, even to competent people (Acts 18:24–26). They met Paul in Corinth and worked with him there as tentmakers (Acts 18:1–4). They then accompanied Paul to Ephesus and were clearly fond of each other's company (Acts 18:18–21). The friendship stood the test of time, as Paul continued to send greetings to them (1 Corinthians 16:19, 2 Timothy 4:19).

FOLLOWERS

Paul had many Followers. However, Titus and Timothy seemed to be especially close, with Paul describing both as 'my son' (Titus 1:4, 2 Timothy 2:1). Paul even boasts of Timothy that 'as a son with his father he has served with me in the work of the gospel' (Philippians 2:22).

FOLK

In Paul's eyes, Mark transitioned from being a Friend to Folk, because Mark had deserted him during a missionary trip. As a result, Paul didn't think it wise to take Mark with him on the following trip (Acts 15:38). Interestingly, it appears Paul went on to change his mind about Mark, as he later requested his help (2 Timothy 4:11). People don't have to stay in a particular category forever; they may move between them.

FOE

Paul suffered under many of these (2 Corinthians 11:23–26). His scariest-sounding Foe has to be 'Alexander the metalworker', who did Paul 'a great deal of harm' (2 Timothy 4:14).

HOW DO I APPLY IT?

Just as a fire needs heat, fuel and oxygen to physically ignite, so followers of Christ need prayer, the Word and people to spiritually ignite. Long-term spiritual growth cannot happen without others; it's not how we're designed.

God does and will continue to use all five categories of these relationships in our spiritual growth. Indeed, continuing to love Folk and Foe can be a refining process in itself. However, just as you need to be intentional about using your time for prayer and Scripture, you also need to be intentional about using your time for relationships that will lead to spiritual growth in you and others.

If you aren't directing your spare time towards relationships that are growing you and others as demonstrated in the diagram, you end up being directed by the demands of others. So, applying this entails considering whom you spend your time with, hence the longer list of questions for reflection.

QUESTIONS FOR REFLECTION

Do you have Fathers and Mothers in your life?

Could you seek out a Father or Mother in a certain aspect of growth you need – for example, someone ahead of you in Scripture knowledge, financial management or family care?

Who are your Friends?

Who are your Followers?

Do you have any Foes?

Are there Folk and Foes taking up too much of your time?

Have some of the people you relate to changed categories? For example, have some Friends become Folk?

GO FURTHER

Read *True Friendship* by Vaughan Roberts.[15]

Out of the Comfort Zone

THE CHALLENGE GRAPH
ANDY

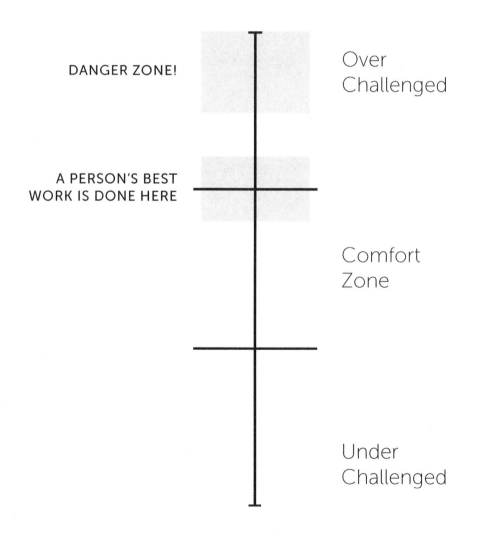

DANGER ZONE!

Over
Challenged

A PERSON'S BEST
WORK IS DONE HERE

Comfort
Zone

Under
Challenged

SETTING THE SCENE

I've done quite a lot of things over the years that have pushed me out of my comfort zone. Signing up for white collar boxing was one of them. It was a grey autumn evening when I first entered the boxing gym, housed in some sweaty railway arches in the East End of London. With no fighting experience, I immediately felt out of my comfort zone. In just eight weeks I would be walking out for my first proper boxing bout with a crowd of 1,500 spectators.

There was one night, three weeks in, when I almost pulled out. That night we had been doing some 'light sparring', and the big brawny guy I was up against seemed to have misunderstood the term 'light'. He threw heavy punches at me, and I threw some right back. We were so appalling at blocking that we both took a number of big blows to the head. That night I went home with a black eye and a headache.

Two days later, it was time to return to the boxing gym for the next training session, and I seriously questioned going back. The previous session had shaken me, but I mustered up the confidence to return, thinking I wouldn't have to spar with the same guy again. Next time I would choose a sparring partner that was smaller than me!

But as I arrived, the coach barked the orders, 'Right, same partners as Tuesday. We're going to continue sparring.' And my heart dropped.

The same brute of a guy walked up to me, but to my surprise he said, 'Mate, I've had headaches the last couple of days since we sparred. Can we go easy tonight?'

'Sure thing,' I replied casually.

Overall, I thoroughly enjoyed the boxing experience. I grew in so many ways, learning a new discipline and attaining new levels of fitness, but that one night of being dangerously over challenged meant I almost gave up. Interestingly, my coach told me that 70 per cent of people who initially sign up to white collar boxing never follow through with the actual fight.

WHAT'S THE BIG IDEA?

We tend to either underestimate or overestimate our limits. This diagram helps us articulate whether we are being suitably challenged. It helps in terms of our work and vocation but also in other areas of life, such as sporting challenges and discipleship. The graph is broken down into three segments.

OVER CHALLENGED

This is where you are out of your comfort zone and feeling very challenged.

At the top end you feel completely overwhelmed, and this is a dangerous zone to be in. You can't operate in this zone for long. The longer you try to operate here, the less effective you become. If you try to work in this Over Challenged Zone for too long, you are likely to burn out.

COMFORT ZONE

In this zone, everything is relatively easy. For a season, this zone can be good because you can coast, but you will not be growing and you will not be stretched. You need more challenge to grow.

UNDER CHALLENGED

In this zone, you are most likely bored. You'll probably be counting the hours until home time. Although you're being paid, the lack of challenge will mean your work is unfulfilling. Much like the Over Challenged Zone, but for the opposite reason, you can't remain in this zone for long.

The diagram marks off an area where our 'best work' is done. Note that this is not the Danger Zone! It is in the area where we are being stretched. As we are stretched, we grow and develop. As we noted in the Emotional Energy Matrix (page 32), sometimes we might need to drop into the lower zones for respite rather than always being challenged.

THINKING BIBLICALLY

Throughout the Gospels, Jesus regularly challenges his disciples. I don't think the disciples were ever under challenged. They were continually learning about the Kingdom and discovering more and more about who Jesus was.

In Luke 10, Jesus sends out the seventy-two in pairs to prepare the way for him. They aren't to take a purse or bag or sandals but to eat and drink whatever they are given. And they are to 'Heal those who are ill and tell them, "The kingdom of God has come near to you"' (verse 9).

Can you imagine being one of the seventy-two, visiting new places and having to rely upon the generosity of strangers?

Exciting? Yes. Challenging? Certainly!

Perhaps we haven't made discipleship in our churches challenging enough. But what's interesting is that Jesus doesn't Over Challenge his disciples. They have been with him, and they know the miraculous is possible. They are not sent out alone but in pairs. They have clear instructions of what to do, no matter how people respond.

HOW DO I APPLY IT?

The big takeaway from this diagram is that some challenge is healthy. If we are always operating in our Comfort Zone, we do not grow, but when we move out of this zone and experience appropriate challenge, we are stretched and able to grow.

To apply this diagram, our first step is to assess where we would currently place ourselves.

If we are in the Over Challenged area, then we need to recognise that we can't stay here long. Vanity or fear of asking for help may hold us back, but we need to acknowledge that we can't live here indefinitely. Doing so is likely to leave us irritable, and we may find it hard to sleep or we look for vices to battle through. If you find yourself here, then something needs to change!

If you are in the Comfort Zone, and have been for a while, what can you do to put yourself in a position of stretching and challenge? If you ebb and flow between the Comfort Zone and tipping into the Over Challenged Zone, then that is a good space to be in!

If you are Under Challenged, do you need to make some more significant changes to move out of this zone?

QUESTIONS FOR REFLECTION

Where are you now on this diagram? Where have you been over the last year?

If you are looking to move out of the Over Challenged Zone, what might be some of the next steps?

If you are looking for more challenge, how is it best to do this?

If you have staff that you oversee, where would you rank them on this diagram? How can you best make sure they are in the most fruitful zone?

GO FURTHER

Read *The Ruthless Elimination of Hurry* by John Mark Comer. [16]

First Things First

THE PRIORITY JAR

ANDY

SETTING THE SCENE

I love to surf.

There is something magnetic about the pull of the ocean. Based in London with two young kids, nowadays I rarely get to chase waves as much as I would like. But I still have many friends for whom surfing is their number one priority. In many ways, it actually dictates their entire lives.

The problem with surfing is that, because the waves are so unpredictable, you can't diarise a surf. Even with the latest meteorological mapping resources, waves and surf conditions are notoriously hard to predict more than a week out. And so, for those who want to make sure that they are able to surf whenever there are perfect conditions, they have to pivot their whole lives in that direction.

I have friends who have moved to the coast. I have friends who have moved continents in search of the best coastline! I have friends who have sacrificed careers and jobs they enjoy so that they can don a wetsuit at the drop of a hat to score perfect waves. More than that, I have friends who have lost family and relationships because they have prioritised surfing over everything else, such is the pull of the perfect wave.

When someone is obsessed with something – whether it be surfing or a football team or a career – their priorities begin to shift around it.

WHAT'S THE BIG IDEA?

It's a classic story, and no one is quite sure where it originates.

Picture a crowded classroom with a philosophy professor at the front. In front of her is a large empty glass jar. The professor begins to place large rocks delicately into the jar, and when one of the rocks reaches the top of the jar, she asks the class, 'Is the jar full?'

The students say yes, but then the professor begins adding small pebbles that slide in between the larger rocks, neatly filling in the gaps. Again, the professor asks, 'Is the jar full?'

Just when the students more cautiously agree that the jar is now full, the professor pulls out a bucket of sand and begins to pour it into the glass jar, filling up the remaining space.

Finally, the professor says, 'The jar is now full.' And she goes on to explain that the jar signifies our lives. The large rocks represent the most important things in life, such as your family, your health, your faith, discipling others, the mission God has given you … the things that make your life meaningful.

The pebbles represent social activities and hobbies. These things are important but not critical to a meaningful life. Some of these 'pebbles' change over time and are less permanent.

Finally, there is the sand. The sand represents the filler. These are things like watching box sets, scrolling social media and cleaning the kitchen. They don't give much meaning to your life as a whole and are either tasks that just need to be completed, things we do to relax or are time-wasters!

THINKING BIBLICALLY

Jesus had clear priorities. If we were exploring what his large rocks were, we might think about his overarching mission. He came to earth ultimately to go to the cross. But his priority was also his disciples. We can see in the three years Jesus had with them how heavily he invested in them. Specifically, we see how he spent time with the three: Peter, James and John.

When we think about Jesus' ministry, we can get lost in the excitement of the miracles and the depth of his teaching and miss that one of his key priorities was most definitely time with his Father. Luke 4–6 is packed full of action as Jesus speaks, heals, chooses disciples and challenges injustice. And yet, sandwiched between these stories are three simple verses: 'At daybreak Jesus went out to a solitary place' (Luke 4:42); 'But Jesus often withdrew to lonely places and prayed' (Luke 5:16); and 'One of those days Jesus went out to a mountainside to pray, and spent the night praying to God' (Luke 6:12).

Jesus knew that no matter how busy life got, he had to spend time alone with the Father. As we explore our priorities in life, how do we make sure this remains a priority?

HOW DO I APPLY IT?

If we start by putting sand into the jar, there'll be no room for the rocks or the pebbles. The same is true in our lives – if we spend our time on the small and insignificant things, we will run out of time for the things that matter. For example, when I became a dad, at times I had to prioritise spending time playing with my kids over having a tidy home.

This diagram can help us think on a macro scale about priorities: how we arrange our diary and what we say yes and no to. However, we sometimes need to prioritise the minor things too – the 'fillers', like ironing a shirt for the next day and cleaning the car; otherwise the 'fillers' can become an overwhelming and stressfully long list.

QUESTIONS FOR REFLECTION

If the jar of your life could contain just five large rocks, what would they be? What does it look like to prioritise them in your life?

What would some of the pebbles be? How flexible are they, and how often do they negatively impact your focus on the rocks?

What are some of the sand 'fillers' of life? Do they ever get mis-prioritised?

GO FURTHER

Read *Master Your Time, Master Your Life* by Brian Tracy.[17]

Holding on to Hope

THE CIRCLES OF PRESSURE
CHRIS

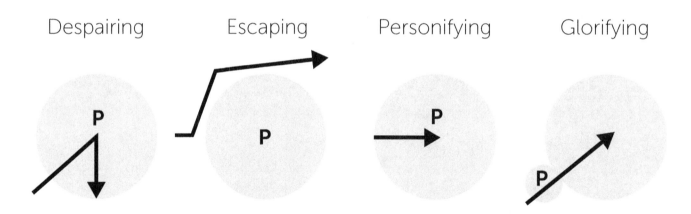

Despairing   Escaping   Personifying   Glorifying

SETTING THE SCENE

In the mid-80s, Simon Yates and Joe Simpson successfully ascended the summit of Siula Grande in the Peruvian Andes, via the almost vertical west face. However, upon the descent they encountered difficulties. Joe suffered a hundred-foot fall, and Simon, holding Joe's support rope over the crevasse, heard nothing and assumed he was dead. Unable to haul him up, with tears in his eyes, he eventually cut the rope. Simon continued the descent, alone and distraught.

By some miracle, Joe regained consciousness and found himself on a ledge. He finally gained enough strength to slowly abseil to the bottom of the crevasse and crawl onto the glacier via a side opening. From there, he spent three days without food and only splashes of water from melting ice, limping and crawling five miles back towards the base camp. Losing a third of his body weight in freezing temperatures, he went almost completely delusional.

It was only when Joe was overwhelmed by a terrible smell that he realised he'd just crawled through the latrine area of the base camp. By this time Simon and the support crew had been scheduled to leave, so Joe said to himself, *This is it. This is as far as this game goes. I'm not capable of going any further*. Tearfully recounting the event in the docu-film *Touching the Void*,[18] Joe says, 'I made the mistake of having a little bit of hope that they would still be there. And when I shouted and they weren't there, I knew I was dead then. That moment when no one answered the call, it was ... a loss, I think. I lost me.'

However, Simon was still there. He heard Joe's last shouts, ran to him, picked him up and brought him into the refuge of the tent.

WHAT'S THE BIG IDEA?

Pressure is a part of life. It can take on many guises: sickness, disappointments, accusations, let-downs. Some pressure will be a consequence of your poor choices, but in a broken world, with broken people, much of it will not.

How and when pressure comes is usually outside of our control, but how we respond to it is not. Indeed, as a leader, how you lead yourself through pressure is perhaps the greatest test of your authenticity. Pressure asks, What are you made of? Do your values really run through you, like the blood in your veins, or are they only superficial and surface-deep? The Circles of Pressure diagram illustrates four responses to pressure: three undesirable and one desirable. The P indicates pressure.

DESPAIRING

This is when we surrender to the pressure we're facing and allow it to have its way with us. Like carrying a rucksack of rocks in the ocean, the pressure eventually pushes us down under its weight. This is depicted in the diagram through the downward arrow.

ESCAPING

This is when we will do anything we can to escape the pressure. Often, people do this by putting on a brave face and denying the power the pressure is having on them. The pressure is not contemplated, explored and shared but buried away, because to face it head-on feels overwhelming.

The good things we enjoy, such as work, sports and food, are often used as escapes, to distract us from the pressure. When we use them this way, they become less the icing and more the cake of life. We do anything we can to ignore our emotions and help avoid passing through the pressure head-on, depicted by the arrow that detours the P.

PERSONIFYING

This is the rarest, but most dangerous, reaction to pressure. Here, we're not despairing of the pressure, or seeking to escape from it, but have set up home within it. No distance between us and the pressure is mapped out; the pressure has become a part of our identity. Rather than thinking, *I'm struggling with this pressure*, we start to believe, *This pressure defines who I am*. This is depicted in the diagram by the arrow remaining in the P.

GLORIFYING

This is the ability to walk through pressure righteously because of an awareness of the hope we have in Jesus. We are able to put one step in front of another, no matter how small, because of the power of hope.

Just as the prisoner endures the pressures of his sentence by hoping for his coming release date, so we are able to endure and even rejoice through pressure, knowing that our heavenly inheritance awaits. This honest but rejoicing posture through pressure glorifies the Hope-giver. This is depicted in the diagram with an arrow that passes through a smaller P, into a larger circle representing the much greater heavenly glory to come.

THINKING BIBLICALLY

Jesus specifically warned us that we will have trouble in this life (John 16:33), and so we shouldn't be surprised (1 Peter 4:12) or naive (2 Timothy 3:1) when pressure comes. Further, being a follower of Jesus will increase pressure in our life, as we follow in the footsteps of a crucified Saviour (Matthew 16:24, Acts 14:22, 2 Timothy 3:12).

The Bible hints at the temptation to face pressure with a Despairing (2 Corinthians 4:8), Escaping (Luke 21:34) and Personifying (1 Peter 2:9–10)[19] approach, and firmly points us to a Glorifying approach, most succinctly summarised in 2 Corinthians 4:17: 'For our light and momentary troubles are achieving for us an eternal glory that far outweighs them all.'

This verse, written by Paul, who experienced phenomenal pressure (2 Corinthians 11:23–29), informs us that in comparison to eternal glory, our trouble, or pressure, is both light and momentary. The pressure may feel incredibly heavy, far beyond our ability to carry. The pressure may feel incredibly long, far beyond our ability to endure. However, if all the weight and time of pressure we face in this life could be put on one side of a set of scales, and our eternal glory with Jesus on the other, the glory side would break the scales and crash through the surface it sat on. There's no comparison.

See also the link in the verse between our troubles now and the glory to come. In some mysterious way we are yet to fully understand, our pressure is achieving an eternal glory for us. This means that a believer's pressure is always meaningful: 'Every millisecond of your misery in the path of obedience is producing for you a peculiar glory because of that.' [20]

So, when the promised pressures come, it's possible to adopt a Glorifying approach, through the perspective-shaping awareness that the pressure we face is not only light and momentary compared to our eternal glory but is also working a glory for us.

HOW DO I APPLY IT?

Apparently, when the seventeenth-century Scottish minister Samuel Rutherford was cast into the cellars of affliction, he was cheered up by remembering that the great King always kept his best wine there.[21] It's in the midst of your pressures that the hope of Jesus tastes the sweetest. Achieving a Glorifying response to pressure therefore depends on your ability to avoid Despairing, Escaping and Personifying, by drinking in afresh the hope of the gospel in the midst of whatever pressure you are facing. So, when you least feel like it, it's likely the best time to remind yourself of truth.

QUESTIONS FOR REFLECTION

Of the four circles, what is your consistent reaction to pressure? Why?

What will help you posture better towards the Glorifying circle?

GO FURTHER

Reflect on the worship song 'Though You Slay Me' – Shane & Shane featuring John Piper: youtube.com/watch?v=qyUPz6_TciY.

Discerning Calling

THE SWEET SPOT

ANDY

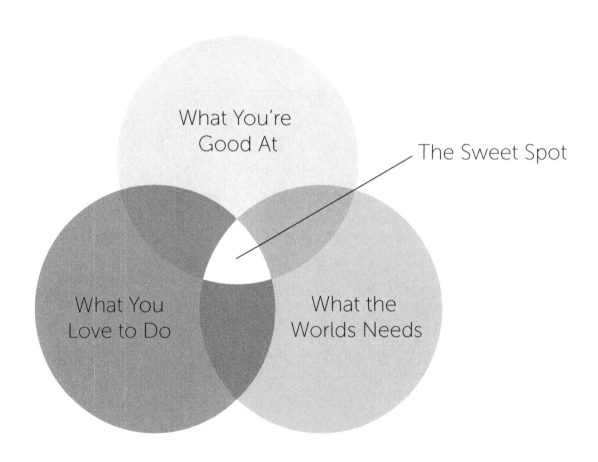

What You're
Good At

The Sweet Spot

What You
Love to Do

What the
Worlds Needs

SETTING THE SCENE

'He who dies with the most toys wins.'

The phrase – accredited to Malcolm Forbes, the American entrepreneur who had a notoriously lavish lifestyle – adorned many sports cars as a bumper sticker in the 1980s. It's a deceitful catchphrase; most of us know that material possessions are not what life is all about.

However, it's amazing how often this mentality can slip into our way of thinking. Over the years, I have met a number of people who hate their jobs and yet are unwilling to leave them. For some of them, there is the fear of the unknown, but for many, moving jobs would mean a pay cut. And a pay cut would mean downsizing. And that feels like losing.

Not everyone has the luxury of chasing a dream career, especially if we have families that are dependent upon us, but with one shot at life, it's important we live it well. Professor of Human Development Karl Pillemer[22] surveyed 1,500 Americans and found that one of their top eight regrets was not taking enough career chances. He found that many of the people he interviewed regretted saying no to opportunities because they were afraid of taking a chance or felt too comfortable in their current job. When we spend so much of our waking lives at work, surely if we hate our jobs, we need to explore what could be different.

WHAT'S THE BIG IDEA?

Discerning what we should do with our lives can be challenging. There are so many different directions we can take. In his classic book *Good to Great*,[23] Jim Collins argues that companies go from being 'good' to 'great' by finding their Sweet Spot, which is finding the intersection of the three questions below:

1. What can you be the best at in the world?
2. What drives your economic engine?
3. What are you deeply passionate about?

The model is used for companies but can also be used by individuals with a slight tweak of the questions:

1. WHAT ARE YOU GOOD AT?
This is an opportunity to list your strengths, your talents and your experience. It's about thinking through what comes easily to you that others might find difficult. You may not enjoy doing all these things, but if you are good at them, then you can still write them down!

As you answer this question, it can be helpful to think through what other people think you are good at and give you compliments for. If you are finding it a tricky question to answer, you might even want to ask family members or colleagues.

2. WHAT PAYS?
This second question is about working out potential income streams. It might be funding you have historically received or potential revenue that you think could be tapped into.

For example, is there a product or service that people might be willing to pay you for? Are there issues you've been able to address in past workplaces that you think you could solve for others? Are there gaps in services you have spotted that you think you could help meet?

3. WHAT DO YOU LOVE TO DO?

List the things in life that bring you joy. It could be certain activities or hobbies you love. It could be subjects and ideas you love to explore and read about. It could be causes that are close to your heart where you want to make a difference.

A great question to help prompt you is: If you never had to work again, how would you spend your time? It's important to note that you don't have to be overly experienced in these areas.

THINKING BIBLICALLY

The Genesis story helps us understand the concept of work. Work is not just something to be endured. It is part of our created purpose. In Genesis 1:26, it is clear that humanity was made in the image of God with a commission to rule over creation, and in Genesis 2:15 there is the mandate to serve and preserve creation.

For Adam and Eve that meant nurturing a family, growing crops, naming animals and managing the garden. As God created the world for human flourishing, we are invited to partner with him today in continuing that narrative. Made in his image, we can play our part in bringing order out of chaos, creating things of beauty, releasing potential and providing for others.

The Genesis story does not end in chapter two, because in chapter three, after the fall, the ground is cursed and 'through painful toil you will eat food from it all the days of your life' (verse 17). This means that work has now been corrupted. Not all we do will be in our Sweet Spot. Our working lives will likely have moments of conflict, boredom and frustration, but seeing our work as more than something that pays the bills is vital. It is part of what it means for us to be human.

HOW DO I APPLY IT?

When I work through this diagram myself, or with someone else, I often draw the three circles and then begin writing some of the things that come to mind for each circle. I normally try to fill in one circle at a time – but do it the way that works best for you.

Once you have everything written down, start to look for the overlaps. There could be some common ideas in two or three circles or some thoughts that overlap. Start noting these down in the Sweet Spot at the centre of the circles. As you do this, think through whether there is a way to shift your present job to be working more from your Sweet Spot. For example, that could involve working fewer hours a week in your current role. Alternatively, it might mean a more radical shift and a change of jobs.

QUESTIONS FOR REFLECTION

How can this tool help you to think through your current role and rhythm?

Who could you invite to help you think this through and reflect on these three areas in your life?

What shifts might you need to make to find more balance in what you invest your time in?

GO FURTHER

Read *Good to Great* by Jim Collins.

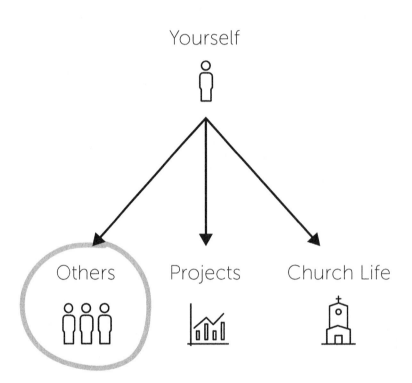

LEADING OTHERS

Having grown in an understanding of yourself and God from the first thirteen diagrams, you've hopefully gained insight in how to relate to others as you lead. That doesn't make leading others easy though. Indeed, even Jesus, leading perfectly from the inside out, got so frustrated at his disciples' lack of faith that he longed to stop leading (Mark 9:19; Matthew 17:17). But he stuck with it, because he knew he was sent to pour himself out into others (Matthew 20:28). So, the next thirteen diagrams are here to keep you out of a silo and effectively lead others for the glory of God.

LEADING OTHERS WITH **UNDERSTANDING**:
Diagrams for Discerning the Heart of Others

LEADING OTHERS WITH **COMMUNICATION**:
Diagrams for Expressing Your Heart to Others

LEADING OTHERS IN **SYNERGY**:
Diagrams for Achieving Collaboration

Perceiving Pain

THE KÜBLER-ROSS CHANGE CURVE
CHRIS

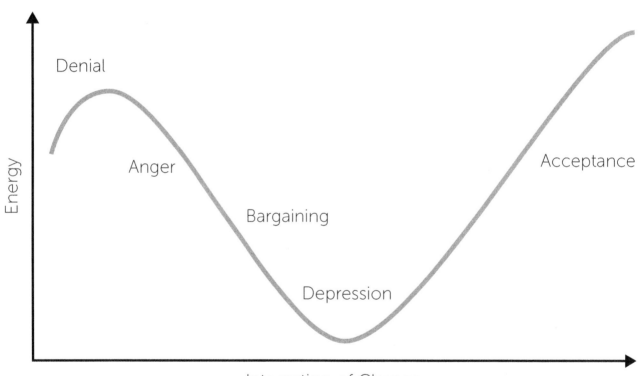

SETTING THE SCENE

I had only been a committed Christian for a year, but somehow I was asked to be part of a prayer response team at a church meeting. A talk was given, a song was sung, and anyone wanting prayer was asked to come forward.

Honestly, I was hoping the dishevelled and malodorous guy who had unexpectedly wandered into the meeting would go to someone else for prayer. But he didn't. Taking a moment to be still and pray, I intuitively felt I should hug the guy. But hugging guys wasn't really what I did back then, so gradually and awkwardly I patted my hand on his back, hoping to communicate that if a hug was what this guy needed, I was willing. He responded, we hugged, and then he started sobbing … a lot. The embrace must have lasted five to ten minutes, with a good amount of snot congealing on my shoulder.

It transpired that this guy had been abusing drugs and was very unwell. Just a week after that embrace, he died. I was informed that his mother, hearing of the hug and a committed Christian herself, stood up at the funeral and recalled this event, announcing she was so glad that her son got to experience Jesus' grace before he died.

Significant loss is a part of life. We experience loss when a parent leaves, a marriage ends or, like the mum in the story, a loved one dies. It happens when a dream of how we see our life going gets completely disrupted. Most significantly, we must all one day, like the guy in the story, face our own death. Despite these realities, we tend to hide or downplay grief and the pain it causes.

WHAT'S THE BIG IDEA?

Elisabeth Kübler-Ross was a Swiss-American psychiatrist who wrote *On Death and Dying* in 1969.[1] In the backdrop of a progressive and modern medical world, where death was subconsciously shrouded by hospitals, her book carefully detailed the voices of those who were dying.

A significant result of the study was the diagram opposite, which went on to achieve vast cultural adoption as a way of understanding grief not only for an individual's death but also for other forms of loss or change in life.

It suggests five observed stages of loss, outlined by the acronym DABDA:

Denial: There's a sense of shock, which makes us think, *This can't be happening.*

Anger: The news has now sunk in a little, and we want to retaliate against it, perhaps thinking, *I'm not going to let this happen.*

Bargaining: A softened anger transpires, where we seek to do anything to minimise or counteract the loss.

Depression: The pain of the loss now takes hold as the consequences are explored.

Acceptance: There is no longer a struggle against the loss, and we may begin to take practical steps to move forward.

The cycle has come under academic scrutiny, much of which has failed to appreciate Kübler-Ross's clarification that this cycle is not intended to be a universal system in which we all follow a chronological grief journey. Most people will experience at least two of these stages, while others may experience all of them. For some, the process will be more like a roller coaster where stages are revisited, while for others, the stages will stall, overlap, occur together or be missed completely. As this is not an observation of a total grief process, other key emotional reactions to loss, such as hope, may also be experienced.

THINKING BIBLICALLY

In John 11:1–44, Jesus' friend Lazarus is at death's door, and his sisters, Mary and Martha, call Jesus to come quickly as 'the one you love is sick'. By the time Jesus arrives, Lazarus has died. Jesus turns up as the funeral is taking place and meets with Martha and Mary. Three of Jesus' reactions to his own and others' grief are significant to note here.

Anger. When Jesus sees Mary and others weeping, we read that Jesus 'was deeply moved in spirit and troubled' (verse 33), and then when at the tomb he was 'once more deeply moved' (verse 38). The Greek language used in these verses draws up images of Jesus being like a horse eager to get into battle, or being churned up like the sea … this is serious anger. Jesus hates death: He never wanted it in his world, and so he is indignant that it has plunged its fangs into his close friend.

Sadness. In verse 35, we read simply, 'Jesus wept' – one of the shortest but most profound verses in Scripture. It literally reads in Greek, 'Jesus burst into tears.' Such love, such pain.

Faith. In verse 39, Jesus says, 'Take away the stone', and then, in verse 43, 'Lazarus, come out!' Lazarus obeys. It's amazing that Jesus experienced deep anger and sadness, emotions found on the Change Curve, despite knowing that just minutes later he would raise Lazarus from the dead. Seeing Jesus go through this range of emotions helps us know that it's okay when we and others experience the emotions of the Change Curve, even though we have the hope of the gospel. Although we don't grieve as the world does (1 Thessalonians 4:13), it is normal and natural to have times of grief (John 16:22).

HOW DO I APPLY IT?

It's important to avoid applying this cycle too simplistically. As leaders we can use it to gain insight into how people may be feeling in a season of grief or change rather than presuming it's a road map all will follow.

If you're aware of an *individual* on your team who is in a season of grief, it's helpful to be aware of the stages. Outside of approaching their own death, the season could be brought on by one of life's five big stressors: the death of someone close, a relationship ending, moving house, a significant illness or the loss of a job. It's your role as a leader to respond compassionately to the needs of your team member by appropriately offering them space, time to talk, guidance and support. It's also good to be aware that those you are leading can subconsciously project their grief feelings onto you. For example, it could be that an individual's anger, expressed in a refusal to talk to you, is a symptom of the grief they are experiencing.

In terms of *group dynamics*, the cycle can be a helpful tool whenever you implement any significant changes. Change affects people's lives and can make those you are leading experience some of the stages of the Change Curve. It's helpful to be aware of these stages and to anticipate that some of those feelings may be expressed or directed towards you as their leader.

QUESTIONS FOR REFLECTION

What significant loss or change have you experienced? Did you experience the stages of the Kübler-Ross curve?

Who in your team right now may be on a journey in the grief cycle?

How might you support them?

GO FURTHER

Read On *Grief and Grieving: Finding the Meaning of Grief Through the Five Stages of Loss* by Elisabeth Kübler-Ross and David Kessler. [2]

Understanding Others

THE PASSIVE LISTENING CURVE
CHRIS

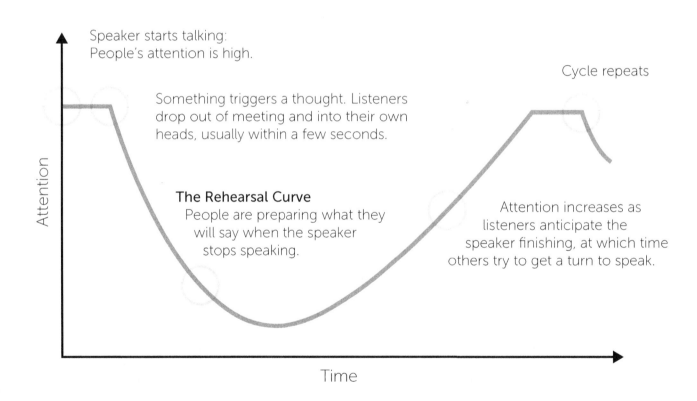

Speaker starts talking:
People's attention is high.

Something triggers a thought. Listeners drop out of meeting and into their own heads, usually within a few seconds.

Cycle repeats

The Rehearsal Curve
People are preparing what they will say when the speaker stops speaking.

Attention increases as listeners anticipate the speaker finishing, at which time others try to get a turn to speak.

Attention

Time

SETTING THE SCENE

Like the child who rushes off to complete an activity before grasping the instructions, we tend to rush off with our own ideas rather than really understand what's being communicated to us.

In leadership training sessions, I'll often teach a few good listening skills, and then ask people to put them into practice by actively listening to each other in pairs. The reactions between these relative strangers around the room are often surprising; they arrange to talk again, share a hug or even cry together.

Good communication is vital, and when it's absent it can have devastating effects. It's been my observation in pastoral work that the greatest threat to a marriage is not sickness, money problems, boredom or even an affair – these are just symptoms of a greater issue: a couple's inability to listen to one another.

WHAT'S THE BIG IDEA?

To draw the best out of those you lead, you need to listen to them. The trouble is, most of us are terrible listeners. The Passive Listening Curve shows a general trend as to how people listen.

Someone starts speaking and the Attention of the listener is high, but quickly (after around six seconds), the Attention drops. Usually this is to think through a thought that the speaker has triggered. The listener then continues to drop quickly into the Rehearsal Curve, where they prepare what they want to say when the speaker stops. The Attention then increases as the listener anticipates the speaker taking a break and their opportunity to speak.

THINKING BIBLICALLY

Have you ever wondered why Jesus told people things about them that he couldn't have naturally known (Mark 2:6–9, John 1:40–42, John 1:47–48, John 4:17–18)? There are many reasons why, but one reason must be that it was an expression of his love. Jesus, by sharing his knowledge of people, opened the curtain to his complete knowing and acceptance of them. To be known and understood gives a person value, significance and meaning. To be known is to be loved. So, one way we can follow this example of Jesus is by listening well, as Scripture encourages: 'everyone should be quick to listen, slow to speak' (James 1:19).

HOW DO I APPLY IT?

Many disengaged team members complain that their team leader doesn't listen. Therefore, if we are to be effective leaders who connect well with those we lead, it's vital to move away from the Passive Listening Curve and instead seek to improve our listening skills. Here are some tips for modelling active listening:

- Avoid distractions: put the phone away!
- Find somewhere quiet.
- Use around 60 per cent of eye contact: much more and you could look intimidating; much less and you could look distracted.
- Try mirroring your body language to the speaker's, and slightly lean in.
- Encourage the speaker with occasional nods and mm-hmms.
- Ask open-ended questions to help the speaker clarify what they're saying, rather than questions that distract or challenge them. For example, 'How did it make you feel when …?'
- Try to feel the feelings they are expressing, and swallow yours up, especially if you're feeling defensive.
- If you think they have finished, allow a few moments of silence; more may come.
- Ask if there is anything else they want to say on the subject.
- Rephrase what has been said back to them.

Creating a culture where everyone in your team is listened to will not only make individuals feel valued but will also strengthen the team and allow people to share their ideas. You may need to gently quieten the oversharers and encourage the silent. You could even pass around a wooden spoon for a week or two of team meetings; whoever is holding it, holds the floor.

You could also lead your team in a listening exercise, pairing them up, sharing the tips above and asking them to take turns to share what they have done in the last week. Then invite feedback for how it felt to be listened to well.

QUESTIONS FOR REFLECTION

Today, is there someone you could commit to try and listen well to?

What are some barriers to you listening well?

How could you foster a culture of listening well in your team?

GO FURTHER

Read *You're Not Listening: What You're Missing and Why It Matters* by Kate Murphy.[3]

The Persecutor, the Victim and the Rescuer

THE DRAMA TRIANGLE

ANDY

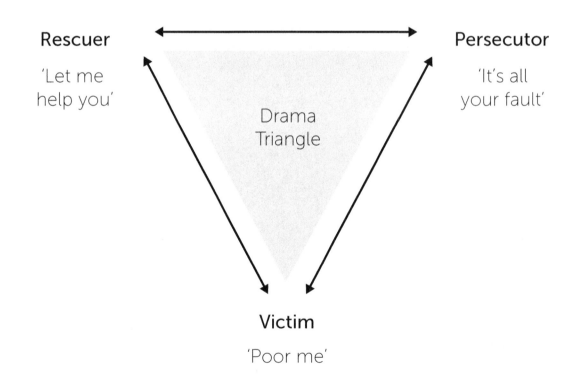

SETTING THE SCENE

Growing up, every Christmas my parents would invite families to our house, and we would always play 'Murder in the Dark'. The game involves turning all the lights off and a pre-decided 'murderer' has to tiptoe around, choosing who to murder. Shortly afterwards the lights go on, and a 'detective' has to ascertain what has happened and guess who the murderer is.

This tradition has continued, and each year at my house we host a Christmas party that has become infamous in our community. Twenty children aged between four and twelve, along with a host of adults, disperse around the house as it is plunged into darkness. Chants of 'one more game' ricochet around the rooms, and each round of the game becomes a little more dramatic, with blood-curdling screams and detectives acting like Miss Marple as they investigate.

Although 'Murder in the Dark' is fun, when it comes to leading teams, we'd prefer much less drama. We want to avoid the petty squabbles and power plays which can jeopardise us achieving our goals.

WHAT'S THE BIG IDEA?

Psychiatrist Stephen Karpman devised the Drama Triangle in the 1960s to illustrate the power games we play in social interactions – within families, communities and the workplace. He explains three roles people adopt: the Victim, the Rescuer, and the Persecutor.[4]

The Victim is at the bottom of the triangle because they don't take responsibility and believe they are powerless in conflict. The Rescuer and Persecutor are at the top points of the triangle because they take responsibility and have power in their relationship with the Victim.

The Victim can be summed up with the expression, 'Poor me'. They may not be an actual victim but perceive themselves to be. They adopt a passive role, failing to take responsibility, and often believe they are in a helpless and hopeless situation, which cannot be changed.

The Rescuer can be summed up with the expression, 'Let me help you'. They have good intentions and want to help the Victim. They regularly intervene to help protect and save the Victim from harm. They are unable to stand by and watch people struggle. By taking on this role, they sometimes avoid their own issues and often feel good about themselves when people become dependent upon them. If their help fails to achieve change for the Victim, they can end up becoming Persecutors.

The Persecutor can be summed up with the expression, 'It's all your fault'. Persecutors have set boundaries and a clear understanding of what is right and wrong. They are strict and need to win arguments at any cost.

Victims often blame Persecutors (or a specific situation) for their problems.

Victims look for Rescuers to help solve their problems for them.

Rescuers look for ways to help Victims.

Rescuers view Persecutors as bullies who aren't willing to help.

Persecutors blame the Victims for their problems without offering help.

Persecutors criticise Rescuers for bailing victims out.

In different scenarios we can take on different roles. Sometimes we play these roles consciously and sometimes unconsciously. In the course of one conflict, we may change roles. For example, the Persecutor's authoritarian and angry stance may cause a negative reaction from the Rescuer and the Victim. They may both blame the Persecutor who may in turn become defensive, thereby switching roles to become the Victim.

All three roles are negative ways of resolving conflict. If the Victim isn't empowered to act, they will remain trapped and dependent on a Rescuer. If a Rescuer fails to empower the Victim, they aren't really helping them. They can become burnt out from rescuing other people. A Persecutor can be overly critical. They can leave the Victim struggling and, at worst, end up acting as a bully.

THINKING BIBLICALLY

In Luke's Gospel, we have a perfect example of a Drama Triangle emerging. Jesus is visiting the home of Mary and Martha (Luke 10:38–42). One sister, Martha, gets busy serving their guests while the other, Mary, sits at the feet of Jesus.

Martha takes up the role of Persecutor when she comes to Jesus asking, "'Lord, don't you care that my sister has left me to do the work by myself?'" At this moment Martha is looking for Jesus to take her side against Mary. By doing so, Mary would become the Victim.

Jesus has a choice to make.

He could side with Martha and also become a Persecutor. Or he could act as a Rescuer and step in to defend Mary's choice.

Instead, Jesus steps outside of the triangle.
He doesn't allow the destructive cycle to develop.

He says, "'Martha, Martha … you are worried and upset about many things, but few things are needed – or indeed only one. Mary has chosen what is better, and it will not be taken away from her.'"

Jesus doesn't take on the role of Rescuer for Mary; instead, he simply affirms Mary's choice. But Jesus also doesn't become the Persecutor of Martha. He comes alongside her, acknowledging the trouble in her heart. His words help offer her a better way as he challenges the distractions. Jesus powerfully navigates the possible Drama Triangle and speaks poignantly into the sibling rivalry.

HOW DO I APPLY IT?

First and foremost, the Drama Triangle will make you more aware of what is happening when conflict arises. People generally have a primary role they will play when they enter into Drama Triangles. It may be that you, as a leader, slip into one of the roles.

As you lead teams, look for this power dynamic at work – identify patterns in interactions and change your own role within them. You could talk the Drama Triangle through as a team and ask people to identify which role they normally adopt. The challenge is to help people move out of those roles.

If we tend to take on the role of Victim, then we need to shift our role to that of *Survivor*. This begins by acknowledging that we are not powerless. Understanding what we want and celebrating what is going well will help us move into this role.

If we tend to take on the role of Rescuer, then we need to shift our role to that of *Coach*. Our purpose is not to solve other people's problems for them but to help coach them so that they can be empowered to move forward themselves. Rather than seeking to fix the issue, Coaches ask, 'What do you think you can do to change this?'

If we tend to take on the role of Persecutor, then we need to shift our role to that of *Challenger*. Challengers are firm but fair, offering constructive feedback and helping people understand the consequences of their actions.

QUESTIONS FOR REFLECTION

Now you are aware of the Drama Triangle, which role are you most likely to take on: Victim, Rescuer or Persecutor?

What might be your next steps in moving out of that role?

Can you identify which roles your team members may naturally take?

GO FURTHER

Read more at karpmandramatriangle.com.

Being Proactive

THE CIRCLES OF CONTROL
ANDY

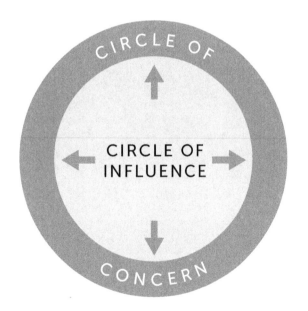

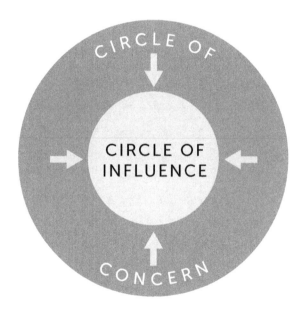

Proactive Focus
Positive energy enlarges
Circle of Influence

Reactive Focus
Negative energy reduces
Circle of Influence

SETTING THE SCENE

The shouting woke my kids up, and my eldest came downstairs with a bemused look upon her face. 'What's happening?'

'Nothing,' I replied. 'Go back to bed.'

'But I heard shouting,' she persisted.

At that point she turned to the TV and saw that the England Euros football match was playing, and I began to feel rather guilty. My frustrated sofa shouts – watching England get knocked out of yet another major football championship – had woken the kids … again.

At 10.30 p.m. it's hard to explain to your child why you were shouting at an England team through the TV screen who were playing a match in another country. My passionate cries of 'Shoot!' were clearly making no impact on the match.

WHAT'S THE BIG IDEA?

Stephen Covey's groundbreaking book *The 7 Habits of Highly Effective People* explores the idea of two circles.[5] The outer circle, the Circle of Concern, encompasses all that concerns us – everything from what we might have for dinner through to climate change. Within this circle is the Circle of Influence, which contains the things that we can impact through the decisions we make. Some things we have direct control over. For example, we can normally determine what we eat, how often we exercise and how regularly we pray. Other things we do not have direct control over, but we can influence. Then there are many things that concern us that we have little influence over whatsoever.

The diagram helps us to understand what we can and can't influence and helps us to identify whether we tend to be Reactive or Proactive in our approach.

Proactive people focus on what we *can* do and what we *can* influence.

Reactive people focus on what we *can't* do and what we *can't* influence – the things beyond our control, such as the weather, pandemics, the economy and whether England will ever win a major championship.

Covey argues that focusing on the things that are beyond our Circle of Influence is a waste of energy. If we choose to focus our energy and effort on what we *can't* change, our Circle of Influence will actually shrink, as we tend to become more negative and frustrated. Reactive people can end up feeling like victims, blaming the world for the challenges they face.

However, if we focus on what we *can* do, we will find our Circle of Influence starts to increase as others perceive us to be effective and are more likely to ask us for help or input.

THINKING BIBLICALLY

As Christians, we might be tempted to reject this model because there is a sense that we can impact anything and everything through prayer. We can pray for all kinds of things that are outside of our influence! We can, and should, pray for the things over which we have no control. However, this model can still be helpful because it helps us intentionally focus our energy and effort on the areas God has given us to influence.

When imprisoned, the apostle Paul is a brilliant example of focusing on what he could do rather than what he couldn't. Although he was no longer in control of his travel plans, he was still able to write letters that not only had an influence on the recipients at the time but also on the church today. In his letter to the church in Philippi, he writes:

Now I want you to know, brothers and sisters, that what has happened to me has actually served to advance the gospel. As a result, it has become clear throughout the whole palace guard and to everyone else that I am in chains for Christ. And because of my chains, most of the brothers and sisters have become confident in the Lord and dare all the more to proclaim the gospel without fear. (Philippians 1:12–14)

Paul was Proactive rather than Reactive. Even though he was imprisoned, he didn't focus on what he couldn't humanly change but used the influence he had to share the gospel and write a chunk of the New Testament!

HOW DO I APPLY IT?

This tool can be helpful when coaching team members who feel overwhelmed. It can help people to discern what is in their remit to influence and what is out of their control. It can be a freeing activity to think through what we are responsible for and what we are not responsible for, and it can also shift attitudes. For example, someone you are coaching may not be able to stop working with a colleague who is frustrating them, but they are able to change their attitude and explore ways to forge a better relationship with them.

It is also a powerful tool for teams. As you consider this diagram collectively, you will find you have a much wider Circle of Influence. When starting a new project or initiative, it can be helpful to take a large sheet of paper and draw a big circle on it, labelled 'Circle of Concern'. You can ask team members to write down their areas of concern on Post-it notes in the circle.

Once this has been done, draw a second circle in the middle of the first circle and label it 'Circle of Influence'. You then arrange the Post-it notes on the diagram into things you can influence and things that are outside of your direct influence. The team often realises they can influence more than they initially thought.

The Post-it notes outside of your direct influence are the things to pray about, and the Post-it notes in the inner circle are the things to prayerfully get to work on.

QUESTIONS FOR REFLECTION

Do you focus primarily on things in the Circle of Concern that you can't directly influence or on the things in your Circle of Influence?

Who and what is in your Circle of Influence?

What can you do to expand your Circle of Influence?

GO FURTHER

Read *The 7 Habits of Highly Effective People* by Stephen Covey.

Relate, Listen and Then Share

THE FEEDBACK SEE-SAW

CHRIS

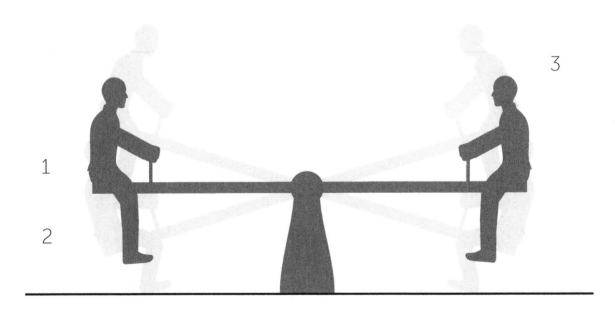

SETTING THE SCENE

The Emperor's New Clothes, written by Hans Christian Andersen, finishes with the emperor walking proud in a procession before a whole town, completely naked. The problem? The emperor's clothes were made from a fabric that was supposedly only invisible to those who were unfit for office or unusually stupid.

The result? Everyone was afraid to give the emperor the feedback he desperately needed. When a child eventually points out that he's naked, and the whole town finally agrees, it's too late and the emperor carries on regardless.

We often dis-serve others by failing to give the critical feedback they need, usually out of fear. Conversely, we allow our blind spots to evolve if others are afraid to give us the feedback we need.

When I worked on my first media job, I was abruptly sat down by a senior journalist. For nearly half an hour she shredded my report to pieces, only eventually stopping when she saw tears well up in my eyes. My confidence was knocked for weeks, if not months.

By contrast, a fellow pastor once made me a coffee, asked how I was, and then gently brought up a couple of blind spots he'd seen in my preaching. It wasn't easy to hear, but I still heed those corrections today, and I'm a better leader as a result.

WHAT'S THE BIG IDEA?

Giving and receiving honest feedback with those who you live and work with is essential to ensuring continued improvement. Without a culture of feedback, errors are repeated and frustrations are allowed to fester. The See-Saw diagram outlines a simple and memorable three-step process for giving effective feedback.

1. Relate. The see-saw starts flat. You (on the left), and the person or persons you are giving feedback to (on the right), are level. This must be the foundation of feedback: One human, created in the image of God, is speaking to another human(s), also created in the image of God. Too often feedback is given instantly and/or irritably, doing more damage than good.

2. Listen. The see-saw beam first lowers left on the pivot. You (on the left), bend your knees, to allow an elevated position to the person(s) you want to give feedback to. This is the most critical yet most forgotten stage. Before providing feedback, even if you have been directly asked to give it, first ask for the other person's perspective on the issue at hand.

3. Share. The see-saw beam now switches, and the right side lowers on the pivot. Having had their perspective listened to, the other person(s) is now more receptive to your perspective. Here is your opportunity to share those things that will ultimately strengthen that person(s).

After this three-step process, you're ready to repeat the process until the conversation is satisfactorily finished. Specifically, you Relate again, Listen to the other person's perspective, then Share your feedback appropriately, before repeating if necessary.

THINKING BIBLICALLY

To some extent we are all 'pleaseaholics'; we care about what others think of us, and so crave, in some measure, for them to be pleased with us. The root of this is good. What kind of person would want everyone to be displeased with them? Indeed, Paul said, 'I try to please everyone in every way' (1 Corinthians 10:33). However, this becomes a problem when this desire to please prevents us from taking valuable action, such as giving feedback. Therefore, the first hurdle to applying the Feedback See-Saw diagram is getting on the see-saw.

Knowing that appropriate feedback is a service to others (Proverbs 26:24–28, 27:6, 28:23, 29:5) helps us get onto the see-saw, break through our 'pleaseaholic' status and paradoxically say with Paul, 'If I were still trying to please people, I would not be a servant of Christ' (Galatians 1:10). Scripture also helps inform our approach in the three-step process.

1. Relate. When Paul wanted to confront Peter for the way he refused to eat with Gentiles, he 'oppose[d] him to his face, for what he did was very wrong' (Galatians 2:11 NLT). To relate well, we need to follow suit and, as a general rule for serious feedback, give it face-to-face.

When Jesus confronts Peter's denial on the shore of Galilee, he first cooks him a fish breakfast, before taking him to one side and raising the issue (John 21:9–17). Good leaders intuitively do the same; they ensure the basic needs of their followers are met before offering feedback.

2. Listen. Rushing straight into your feedback can make you look stupid: 'Fools find no pleasure in understanding but delight in airing their own opinions' (Proverbs 18:2). By genuinely listening first, you may find there's a 'plank in your own eye' (Matthew 7:4) or a different perspective that you hadn't yet seen. No wonder Francis of Assisi prayed, 'O Divine Master, Grant that I may not so much seek … to be understood as to understand.'

3. Share. 'Wounds from a friend can be trusted' (Proverbs 27:6) and even desired because 'iron sharpens iron' (Proverbs 27:17). Therefore, by 'speaking the truth in love, we will grow to become in every respect the mature body of him who is the head, that is, Christ' (Ephesians 4:15).

HOW DO I APPLY IT?

Once you're on the see-saw, it's a case of intelligently applying the see-saw process.

1. Relate. Seek to relate to the other person by affirming their value. Separate the behaviour or issue you want to address from them as a person; they are more than this mistake.

2. Listen. By raising the subject, but asking for the person's perspective first, helpful outcomes can follow, such as:

- The person raises their mistake, saving you the awkwardness of having to raise it yourself. It's amazing how aware people can be about the mistakes they make.
- You find you have misread the mistake and failed to appreciate mitigating circumstances.
- You discover you're somewhat to blame, and there's some helpful feedback for you to take on board.

It's important to apply active listening here, as outlined in the Passive Listening Curve diagram (see page 74). Once complete, like a see-saw, the conversation should naturally bounce back to you, and you're ready to share.

3. Share. This isn't your turn to let loose; it's time to gently and specifically feed back on the issue you want to address, so thinking beforehand about what you're going to say is helpful. This can obviously be updated to incorporate any new information you've gleaned. You may want to use the following framework: 'I now understand that you did *w* because of *x*. However, when you did *w*, it made me feel *y*. In the future I'd appreciate it if you did *z*.'

If you're giving more general feedback, it's obviously important to highlight the positives as well as the negatives. But beware of relying on the 'praise sandwich', where you cushion the issue with positives, as this can often camouflage the issue and cause confusion.

Unless feedback is encouraged by creating time and space for it to be shared, you can find yourself trapped in a positive feedback loop, much like the emperor in the story, in which no one feels at liberty to be honest with you.

QUESTIONS FOR REFLECTION

What feedback have you received that has served you well?

How did you feel about it at the time? And now?

Is there someone you could serve by arranging to give them feedback using the See-Saw process?

GO FURTHER

Read *Crucial Conversations: Tools for Talking When Stakes are High* by Kerry Patterson.[6]

More Than Words

MEHRABIAN'S FORMULA OF COMMUNICATION

ANDY

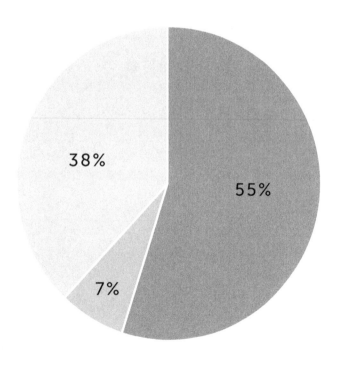

7% Spoken Words

38% Tone of Voice

55% Body Language

SETTING THE SCENE

I'm normally pretty bad at celebrating my wife's birthday, but the year she turned forty, I decided to go all out. Forty felt significant.

One of the things I decided to do was to buy her forty presents. I began shopping in earnest two months out and set up a separate Amazon account, so she wouldn't know what I was up to. Now, coming up with forty presents is difficult, especially the last ten. How many chocolate bars can one woman get for her birthday?

Her birthday finally arrived, and the kids thought it would be a good idea to hide all the presents around the house. Each one had a little note attached to it affirming something about her. And so alongside breakfast in bed, a little birthday treasure hunt was set.

It was interesting to watch her open each present. Some of the gifts she genuinely liked, but then there were others she seemed less keen on. Phrases like, 'Oh Andy, this is a lovely gift. Thanks so much!' seemed authentic on the surface, but the look on her face told a different story. There was one gift in particular, a pair of slippers that I thought were pretty on trend, that got the response, 'Oh, these are … err … great.' And straight away I knew she hated them. Words never tell the whole story.

WHAT'S THE BIG IDEA?

When we look at the pie chart, it's interesting to note that only 7 per cent of our communication is conveyed through the actual words we say.

This is Mehrabian's Formula of Communication.[7] But before we delve into this formula, it's important to note that this is one of the most misquoted formulas out there!

The formula was devised from studies involving speakers who were talking about their feelings and attitudes. The formula picks up on the incongruence between words and expression – where the words being spoken don't match the tone or the facial expressions. In these case studies, the listener believed what they saw rather than what they heard.

This formula was not designed to explain all communication. For example, when a police officer tells you to get out of your vehicle, you do as you are told. You don't try to read her body language to look for deeper meaning. And if a lecturer is delivering a talk on biblical hermeneutics at a university, they need to spend the majority of their time preparing what they will say, not on the tone with which they will say each line.

So why have we included this diagram? Although this formula does not provide a catch-all for every communication situation, it powerfully illustrates the importance of non-verbal and body language in communication, both when we are speaking and when we are listening. Leaders need to be able to understand the difference between words and meaning if they are to lead well.

The key take-home is that words alone don't constitute communication.

THINKING BIBLICALLY

When we think about how Jesus communicated, we straight away think about his teaching and his parables. We can easily skim the familiar stories and miss that Jesus also communicated effectively through tone and body language.

Jesus extends his hands and touches the leper (Luke 5:13). He lays his hands on the children to bless them (Matthew 19:15). With the daughter of Jairus, he takes the girl's hand (Mark 5:41). He washes his disciples' feet (John 13:5–9). He looks to heaven as he feeds the five thousand and blesses the loaves and fish (Matthew 14:19). He stands to read from Isaiah in Nazareth (Luke 4:16) and sits to expound it (Luke 4:20).

Jesus sighs (Mark 7:34) and groans (John 11:33 NKJV), and weeps (Luke 19:41) and calls out, 'he who has ears to hear, let him hear' (Luke 8:8). And as he ascends to heaven, he lifts his hands and blesses the disciples (Luke 24:50).

HOW DO I APPLY IT?

As leaders, it's important that we understand what we're communicating and who we are communicating with. With that in mind, we need to communicate intentionally.

First, think through who you communicate with in any given week; for example, staff, volunteers, accountants or trustees.

Think through the ways in which you communicate; for example, presentations, conversations, video conferencing, phone calls and written correspondence such as emails and social media.

Bearing in mind the learning from Mehrabian's Formula and the fact that you cannot convey tone with written text, are you using the best means of communication for the different people you are speaking with each week?

Second, explore how you can help those you work with to improve communication. For example, if team members give talks and presentations, can you invite everyone to give each other feedback on tone and body language afterwards?

QUESTIONS FOR REFLECTION

How much do you naturally observe tone and body language?

When was the last time you significantly miscommunicated with someone?

On reflection, how might the insights from Mehrabian's Formula have helped?

GO FURTHER

Read *Silent Messages: Implicit Communication of Emotions and Attitudes* by Albert Mehrabian.

Handling Disagreement

THE CONFLICT CASTLE

CHRIS

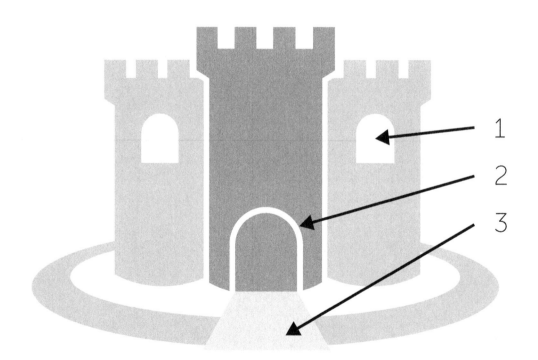

SETTING THE SCENE

By picking up a holiday hire car a few miles down the road from the airport, I managed to obtain a swish car for the same price as a basic one. I quickly grew accustomed to all the swanky features, except one: the auto-steer. I'd be happily travelling along the road when what felt like the forceful action of a ghost moved the steering wheel to align itself to the centre of the road, without any thought or direction from me. As I am usually a confident driver, my kids continually chuckled at my ensuing flapping.

When it comes to how you handle conflict, you will have an auto-steer function, conditioned by the way you are wired and the experiences you have had. When a disagreement arises, your auto-steer subconsciously kicks in, and you may lose control of the wheel. You handle the disagreement in the same way you always have, often resulting in the conflict following a path you don't want it to. The Conflict Castle diagram seeks to alleviate that reliance upon your auto-steer and get your hands directing the wheel again.

WHAT'S THE BIG IDEA?

Healthy disagreement and conflict are essential requirements for healthy relationships, but we often fail to handle them well. The Conflict Castle seeks to change that.

There are three labelled elements on the diagram, each personifying a common auto-steer approach to conflict. The idea is that when a potential conflict is making its way towards your castle, you approach it in one of the three caricatured ways.

1. You run to the bedroom (draw the curtains and turn the lights off!). Here, you enter a kind of flight mode, where the idea of an approaching conflict makes you run and/or hide. This approach supposes that if you withdraw quickly enough and for long enough, the conflict will go away, and that by ignoring the conflict you can subversively disempower the one bringing the conflict; from their perspective, it looks like no one is home, so unless they are willing to wait, the conflict will eventually pack up and go away. At least, that's what you hope.

Strength: Relational peace is paramount to you.
Weakness: Superficial peace, without tackling issues, is often accepted.

2. You let down the drawbridge (slowly, but you may pull it back up at a moment's notice). You are willing to talk to the conflict-bringer but only on certain terms. This approach supposes that if you engage with the conflict within controlled parameters, a resolution may be found and the conflict resolved. You may lay down ground rules for the conversation, such as 'We're not bringing emotions into this'; 'I need solid examples'; or 'We must reach a resolution quickly.' By controlling the conflict, you hope it will be quickly resolved and the relationship will remain peaceful.

Strength: Finding the truth and making adjustments.
Weakness: Unwilling to engage emotionally.

3. You charge across the bridge (with your allegorical sword drawn). This is the fight mode, where in your mind, the best form of defence is attack. So, the drawbridge is lowered, and you charge across the bridge to meet the conflict head-on. Thoughts of how you can bring potential counterattacks rush through your head. Emotions often run high as you seek to dominate the conflict and win at all costs.

Strength: Honest and willing to fight for relational depth.
Weakness: Potential for being overbearing.

THINKING BIBLICALLY

As well as having potential pitfalls, all three approaches have valuable strengths. Indeed, Jesus used elements of all three:

1. Run to the bedroom. When accused by the high priest before his death, 'Jesus remained silent and gave no answer' (Mark 14:61). He also then 'made no reply' to Pilate (Matthew 27:14), and upon the cross, 'When they hurled their insults at him, he did not retaliate' (1 Peter 2:23).

2. Let down the drawbridge. When the religious elite tried to catch Jesus out, he would control the conflict, often through the use of questions. Perhaps most masterfully, in Mark 12, when Jesus was asked if they should pay taxes to Caesar, he replied, '"Why are you trying to trap me?"' and then called for a coin before asking, '"Whose image is this? And whose inscription?"' This led up to his mic-drop and drawbridge-closing moment when he said, '"Give back to Caesar what is Caesar's and to God what is God's"' (verses 15–17).

3. Charge across the bridge. Jesus often met conflict head-on; he certainly wasn't passive when he suggested accusers had a plank in their own eye (Matthew 7:3–4), when he called the Pharisees 'a brood of vipers' (Matthew 12:34) and when he 'overturned the tables of the money changers' (Matthew 21:12).

HOW DO I APPLY IT?

Use the following three-step process:

1. Rank the approaches. Which of the three approaches outlined would best describe your style of dealing with conflict?

Once you have ascertained your natural approach, work out how you would rank your use of the other conflict approaches, so that you have a clear first, second and third preference.

2. Use different styles appropriately. In a conflict, you will likely use your preferred approaches in the order you have ranked them. For example, you may first 'run to the bedroom', but if the conflict doesn't go away, you may eventually 'let down the drawbridge', and if there's still no breakthrough, you may finally snap and 'charge across the bridge'. This order will vary according to how you ranked the approaches.

Here's the interesting part: Resolution is usually found when you use the same approach as the person you are in conflict with. For example, you start with your first preference: 'letting down the drawbridge'. However, your partner is 'charging across the bridge', and for however long those two different approaches are used, no resolution can be found. Sensing no agreement forthcoming, you switch to 'charging across the bridge', but counterintuitively, despite some heated conflict, you make progress there because of your similarity of engagement. It's therefore helpful to not only know how you approach conflict but also how those you work and live with approach it.

Instead of allowing your subconscious approach to take control, consider what approach the person has and seek to mirror it. For example, if it appears someone has some conflict with you, but they have a 'run to the bedroom' approach, you may want to gently and affirmingly open a conversation where a conflict can be explored. Charging across the drawbridge could keep that person in the bedroom forever, but by engaging gently, you may get them to open up. Alternatively, if someone is 'charging across the bridge', taking one of the other two approaches could leave that person in a prolonged fight mode, so you may want to match their approach by confidently expressing your opinion.

QUESTIONS FOR REFLECTION

What are the 'autopilot' approaches of those you lead?

What are some further strengths and weaknesses of your own autopilot approach?

How can you ensure you don't subconsciously allow the auto-steer to take control in conflict?

GO FURTHER

An alternative diagram for understanding conflict is the Thomas-Kilmann conflict model that uses a graph to categorise five types of conflict style: Avoiding (like a turtle), Competing (like a shark), Compromising (like a fox), Accommodating (like a teddy bear) and Collaborating (like an owl). See *Thomas-Kilmann Conflict Mode Instrument* by Kenneth Wayne Thomas.[8]

Listening Well

FEEDBACK LOOPS

ANDY

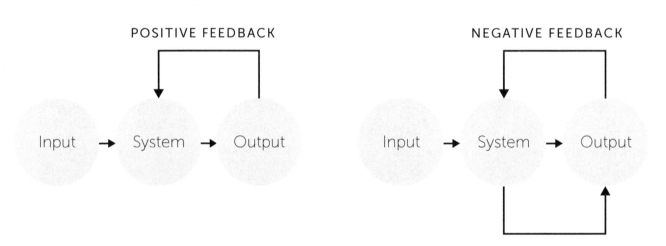

SETTING THE SCENE

There is silence as the new Christian takes to the platform. Their story begins … a search for meaning, purpose and love … with twists and turns. Their life story seems desperate, and the congregation sits in rapt attention. The story continues with a sudden turning point. Something like '… and then I met these Christians.' Or perhaps '… and so I started going on this Alpha course.'

The story ends as the new Christian talks about their transformed life. They finish and hand over the microphone. The congregation applauds, and we celebrate. Our faith is strengthened, and we give thanks for all God has done.

I love these testimonies of people finding faith. But there is another kind of story – one we rarely hear, especially from our church platforms – of people losing faith. It is easy to celebrate what God is doing as people come to faith, but we must also listen to the stories of people who are losing or have lost their faith. We need to understand what has gone wrong so that we can help them rediscover their faith.

A few years back, I spent time meeting with people who used to call themselves Christians. As I listened to their heartbreaking stories, they led me to question, wrestle and grapple with how people lose faith. Some seem to gradually drift away, and others make a definitive break from their Christian beliefs. Some rebel and others just struggle to keep their faith.

One of the threads that ran through their stories was the fact that they had rarely spoken about things early on. Their questions, doubts and uncertainty never had an opportunity to be aired with people of faith. They weren't given space to talk through what they were experiencing in life, and things were left to fester.

As we lead others, whether in a faith context or not, we need to create space for people to share their relevant struggles. Otherwise, they can build up beneath the surface and cause real harm.

WHAT'S THE BIG IDEA?

Feedback loops are found everywhere. They have three components: a System, an Input and an Output. Systems can be macro, such as a country's financial system, or they can be micro, such as a computer system. The input is something that enters the system, and the output is something that happens because of what has been inputted. The output of a system then becomes another input into the system.

There are two kinds of feedback loop: the Negative Feedback Loop and the Positive Feedback Loop. They are found everywhere, including disciplines such as science, health and engineering. More recently, clinical psychologist Jordan Peterson has highlighted and popularised the importance of feedback loops in psychology and societal debate.

The Negative Feedback Loop, contrary to how it sounds, is actually very useful. The loop allows regulation and keeps things at an equilibrium. For example, when the human body gets too hot, we sweat. When we get too cold, our hairs rise to trap an insulating layer of warm air; we shiver, and our blood vessels near the skin's surface constrict. The Input is the change in temperature, the System is our body, and the Output is the action our body takes to stop us from overheating or freezing.

In contrast, Positive Feedback Loops don't self-regulate, and there are no checks and balances. The Input into the system creates an Output that changes the System. In a Positive Feedback Loop, change can be exponential, and a system can become unstable. For example, when fruit ripens, the other fruit in the bowl begins to ripen as well. Ripe fruit produces ethylene, which signals to neighbouring fruit that it is time to ripen. That's why we can end up with a whole bowl of mouldy peaches. This would become a Negative Feedback Loop if the original mouldy peach was removed from the bowl before it spread.

Positive Feedback Loops have been used in psychology to explore cyclical thinking. For example, when a person is anxious about an event, their anxiety negatively impacts the event. That experience reinforces their anxiety, and they become more anxious.

When we are responsible for leading others, this simple diagram highlights the importance of breaking Positive Feedback Loops, giving space to listen and to change what needs to be changed.

THINKING BIBLICALLY

In Mark 3, Jesus is in the synagogue with a man who has a withered hand. Jesus asks, 'Which is lawful on the Sabbath: to do good or to do evil, to save life or to kill?' (verse 4).

The religious leaders are silent. Jesus is angered by their hypocrisy and their hard hearts. He calls the man to stretch out his hand and it is immediately restored.

The Pharisees seemed to live in a Positive Feedback Loop. Jesus was an Input into their System, but they failed to recognise who he was. Over the course of the Gospels, we see their attitudes towards him become so extreme that they have him killed. There are no checks and balances. The same could have happened to Peter and the Apostles in Acts 5 without Gamaliel interrupting the Sanhedrin.

HOW DO I APPLY IT?

This diagram started with the story of people finding and losing faith. For the purpose of this chapter, both sets of people are the System.

The Input is something that has changed. For those finding faith, it may have been the experience of praying or meeting a friend who is a Christian. For those losing faith, the input may have been something like a university lecturer who attacked their faith, or they moved to a new area where they couldn't find a Christian community.

The Output is what happened as a result. For the person finding faith, it may have been going to a church service or joining a house group. For the person losing faith, it may have been reading books that argue for atheism or spending less time with Christians.

Both scenarios can become either Negative or Positive Feedback Loops. They could become a Positive Feedback Loop if there is never any space to hear other opinions. For example, the person finding faith could, in an extreme scenario, stop watching mainstream media, cut off all relationships with non-Christians and move into a commune.

Leaders can help people create Negative Feedback Loops. With the example of someone questioning their faith, we can encourage them to voice their questions and wrestle with tough questions.

There are three parts to the process of moving to a Negative Feedback Loop.

First, you need to identify a feedback loop. This could be a personal, internal mindset, like the example of faith above. Or it could be situational, such as team meetings that fail to stick to their agenda, or someone you lead who regularly misses deadlines.

Second, identify the Input and whether this feedback loop is currently Positive or Negative. Does this feedback loop perpetuate itself (Positive)? Or are there variables that work to change the outcome (Negative)?

Third, analyse and discuss how inputting new variables, or changing the current variables, might result in a Negative Feedback Loop which is more effective.

Creating an environment which encourages the use of Negative Feedback Loops will help those you lead learn how to be more reflective, take in other viewpoints and make the necessary changes to be more effective in their role.

QUESTIONS FOR REFLECTION

What are some of the feedback loops you have seen in those you lead?

Can you identify whether they are Positive or Negative Feedback Loops?

If there are some Positive Feedback Loops, what might you need to do to add some more checks and balances?

GO FURTHER

Read *12 Rules for Life*, chapter 1, by Jordan Peterson.[9]

Team Journeys

KURT LEWIN'S GROUP DYNAMICS
ANDY

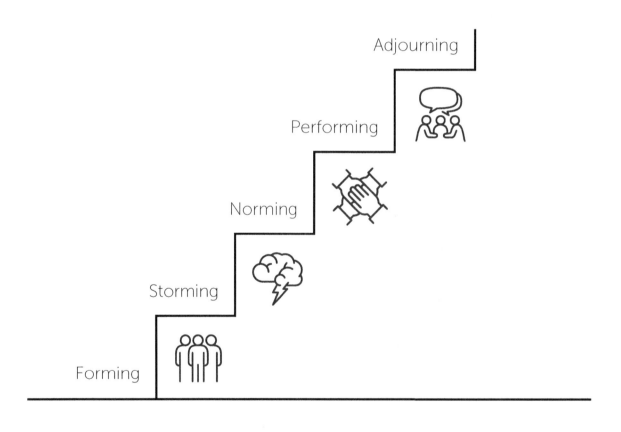

SETTING THE SCENE

In the summer of 2018 twelve boys and their assistant football coach went exploring in the Tham Luang cave in Thailand only to get trapped by an unforeseen rainstorm as the monsoon season struck early.

Their rescue is an incredible story.

Now a blockbuster movie, *Thirteen Lives* tells the story of the rescue operation that filled the world's newsfeeds for weeks on end. What's striking about the story is the variety of people involved in the rescue: the local authorities, the Thai Navy SEALS, paramedics, a number of the world's most experienced divers from the UK and Australia, local volunteers trying to drain the caves and the regional governor offering leadership to the operation.

The film explores the challenges of team dynamics as different factions from different cultures with different perspectives worked together. Few of us will ever have such an intense experience as a team with the stakes so high, but the rescue shows the challenge that team dynamics can pose to all of us in the different seasons of life.

WHAT'S THE BIG IDEA?

In 1965, psychologist Bruce Tuckman wrote a paper titled, 'Developmental Sequence in Small Groups'[10] and coined the phrase 'forming, storming, norming, performing' that is now commonly used in organisations around the world. It's brilliantly simple in helping to explain how teams work.

THE FORMING STAGE

When a new team is formulated, individuals are often thrown together. They may have some idea of why the team exists but will be unsure as to how they fit in and how to relate to others. There might be a whole host of emotions, ranging from anxiety to excitement, as they begin to get to know one another. In this phase they'll be looking to the team leader for guidance on how this team will operate. Forming may take time as individuals ascertain how one another works and as they discern roles and responsibilities. This stage can be testing for leaders!

THE STORMING STAGE

This stage is marked by friction and conflict, often with a lack of agreement when it comes to group decisions. Differing ways of working and different expectations come to the surface. There can be personality clashes, and members of the team may challenge the leader and even the mandate of the team. If things go unresolved, the team can break down. It can result in an undercurrent of resentment and frustration or even face-to-face confrontations with power struggles.

THE NORMING STAGE

Over time, a team moves into a stage where they get to know each other better, and differences are resolved. The leader is respected, and there is appreciation for different people's gifts. Processes and working styles are accepted. The team feels more comfortable around one another, and roles and responsibilities are accepted.

THE PERFORMING STAGE

Then comes the stage in which the team thrives. There is real clarity on why the team exists, and disagreements are resolved agreeably. Goals are achieved as each team member now knows how one another works. In this stage there is more autonomy, and sometimes roles become more fluid as a team works as one.

THE ADJOURNING (OR MOURNING) STAGE

In the 1970s, Tuckman added this stage because all teams eventually disband. For example, a project may end or team members might move on. This is often a challenging season as people mourn the loss of good working relationships.

It's important to note that this process is not always linear. Teams can go back and forth between the different stages. For example, a team that is performing well may have a slight change in personnel and as a result may go back to a Norming or even Storming Stage.

THINKING BIBLICALLY

There are various examples in Scripture of teams, but the most comprehensive insight into a team is Jesus and his disciples. This ragtag group of zealots and Roman sympathisers was going to be rife with friction from its inception. And we see the disciples go through Tuckman's stages.

Forming. The disciples accept the opportunity to follow Jesus. There must have been a sense of excitement as Jesus preached the Sermon on the Mount and spoke powerfully about the Kingdom being at hand. But in this phase, there was little understanding from the disciples about how this vision would be implemented.

Storming. The disciples have various moments of internal conflict. Luke 9:46 showcases the underlying issues: 'An argument started among the disciples as to which of them would be the greatest.' Despite their witness of Jesus' ministry, they also fail to do some of the things they had been empowered to do (Matthew 17:14–21). Jesus has to correct and teach them again and again.

Norming. Things seem to click with the disciples, and when Jesus sends out the seventy-two, they grasp their authority, their role and their mission (Luke 10:17–20). Jesus has empowered his disciples.

Performing. This is most clearly seen in the book of Acts. Jesus has left his disciples physically, but they are empowered by the Holy Spirit. The movement goes global as the disciples release others into their calling, and the impact is multiplied time and time again.

Adjourning. This stage is hard to infer from the text, but when James is murdered by King Herod (Acts 12:2), it would undoubtedly have marked an end to the way things had been.

HOW DO I APPLY IT?

At various points in our lives, we will both be leading teams and be a part of teams. Tuckman's model gives us some language to identify the phases we are going through. It helps us realise how the team is developing both relationally and in terms of confidence in their performance. As leaders it helps us understand how we lead in the different seasons of a team.

Forming. This requires more directive leadership and involves helping team members to set their personal goals and understand how what they do fits in to the overall purpose of the team and the bigger picture. At this stage, leaders also need to create space for team members to get to know one another.

Storming. In this stage, we need to coach, to help the team track progress and set up necessary processes. Building trust is vital, and helping team members to discern what support they need and the support they can offer will build a strong team. We often want to sweep conflict under the carpet, but unless we deal with friction, we can fail to resolve issues and move the team forward.

Norming. During this phase, we need to begin to further empower our team. Regular check-ups on how individuals are doing is important as their progress is reviewed. Continued team building is also important to gel the team together.

Performing. It's important to delegate effectively at this stage. This may involve further development and training for team members. It should also free up some of the leader's time to look for new opportunities.

Adjourning. By the time we reach this phase, we have a pastoral role in helping people finish well. We need to celebrate what has been achieved and affirm people's contributions.

QUESTIONS FOR REFLECTION

Which teams are you presently a part of? Which teams are you leading?

Which stage are each of these teams in? Is your leadership style right for the teams you are leading?

What do you need to do to move each team on towards the Performing Stage or to stay in the Performing Stage?

GO FURTHER

Read *Forming Storming Norming Performing: Successful Communication in Groups and Teams* by Donald B. Egolf.[11]

Teamwork Makes the Dream Work

THE FIVE DYSFUNCTIONS OF A TEAM

CHRIS

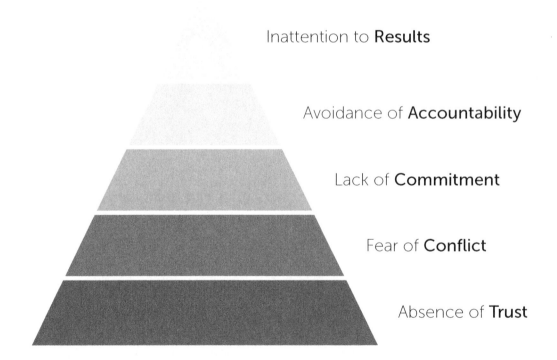

Inattention to **Results**

Avoidance of **Accountability**

Lack of **Commitment**

Fear of **Conflict**

Absence of **Trust**

SETTING THE SCENE

On Tuesday 5 July 2022, over seven hundred MPs, peers and UK church leaders attended the National Parliamentary Prayer Breakfast at Westminster Hall in London. They listened to Reverend Les Isaac OBE speak about the importance of integrity in leadership.

Sajid Javid, Secretary of State for Health and Social Care, was convinced during that speech that he could no longer be part of a team with Prime Minister Boris Johnson. In his own words, 'I made up my mind, went straight back to my office and drafted the resignation letter, and went to see the prime minister later in the day.'[12] This triggered a domino effect of other team members resigning one after the other, culminating in Johnson's resignation just two days later.

Despite Johnson's attempts to exonerate himself from blame, the British public largely perceived him as someone who sought to save his own back,[13] often at the expense of fellow team members. A powerful team, which included some great minds and committed achievers, fell apart because trust had evaporated.

WHAT'S THE BIG IDEA?

In his book *Five Dysfunctions of a Team*, Patrick Lencioni uses a pyramid diagram to illustrate five causes of team breakdown:

1. Absence of Trust: The foundation of trust in a team is essential, and is achieved by vulnerably sharing strengths and weaknesses. Without this trust, teams cannot progress to overcome the second level.

2. Fear of Conflict: Conflict is neither good nor bad but *necessary* to find truth or a clear answer. Without conflict, the team cannot overcome the third barrier.

3. Lack of Commitment: Before accepting a decision, team members need to feel like their input has been respected, or in Lencioni's terms: 'Everyone buys in, when everyone has weighed in.'[14] If a team has a lack of commitment, they cannot attempt to overcome the fourth level.

4. Avoidance of Accountability: When the team are committed, they, and not just the leader, will have the courage to appropriately call out inappropriate attitudes and behaviours. Without that peer challenge, the team cannot progress to overcome the next barrier.

5. Inattention to Results: When each of the dysfunctions is overcome, the team can reach the stage where collective, rather than individual, results are achieved because the team are working together effectively.

THINKING BIBLICALLY

Jesus was the master team builder. From an eclectic and untrained group, he created a team of world changers. He did this, in part, by creating a culture of:

Trust. Jesus did this by openly sharing his sorrow and need for the disciples before the crucifixion (Matthew 26:38). He also showed he trusted his team by delegating tasks to them, such as preparing their Passover meal (Luke 22:8), feeding the five thousand (Mark 6:37) and asking them to do the works he had been doing (Matthew 10:1–8).

Healthy Conflict. Jesus allowed others to express opinions that differed from his own. His disciples would have seen his mother insist Jesus make wine (John 2:1–7), the Centurion suggest an alternative healing approach (Matthew 8:5–13), and the Canaanite woman persist with her request (Matthew 15:21–28).

It's no surprise, therefore, that we see them openly express frustration at not knowing where he was (Mark 1:37), exasperation at being asleep during a storm (Mark 4:38), and consternation at his predicted death (Matthew 16:22).

Commitment. Jesus called his team to a high bar of commitment, asking them to leave everything (Luke 18:22). When other followers left, his team stayed (John 6:67–69). As is inevitable when working with fallen human beings, the whole team didn't stay intact, with Judas betraying Jesus (John 6:70–71). However, it is widely believed that ten of the twelve disciples went on to pay the ultimate price of commitment: martyrdom.

Accountability. Jesus intervened when his team-mates exhibited inappropriate attitudes and behaviours, fulfilling his own command to confront wrongdoing (Matthew 18:15). For example, he challenged the team's argument over who would be the greatest (Luke 9:46–48), corrected Peter's rebuke (Matthew 16:23) and predicted Judas' betrayal (Matthew 26:20–25).

Results. Despite failures (Matthew 17:17) and setbacks (Mark 14:50), Jesus' team was ultimately effective. With the Spirit's help, Jerusalem would never be the same again, as they built a deep and wide Kingdom community (Acts 2:41–47, Acts 4:4), which filled the city with its teaching (Acts 5:28).

HOW DO I APPLY IT?

Applying the principles of the pyramid is fairly self-evident, but it's helpful to know that Absence of Trust can be addressed by creating spaces where team members can vulnerably share about themselves, perhaps using elements of the Johari Window (see page 6), the Iceberg of Emotional Health (see page 40) or the Emotions Wheel (see page 44). Fear of Conflict can be addressed by looking at the Conflict Castle (see page 94), and Avoidance of Accountability can be worked on by applying the Feedback See-Saw (see page 86).

QUESTIONS FOR REFLECTION

What's been the best team you've been a part of?

What was it about that team that was so good?

What's the most significant dysfunction you're aware of in a team you're currently part of?

GO FURTHER

Read *The Five Dysfunctions of a Team: A Leadership Fable* by Patrick M. Lencioni.[15]

The Ideal Team Player

HUMBLE, HUNGRY AND SMART

ANDY

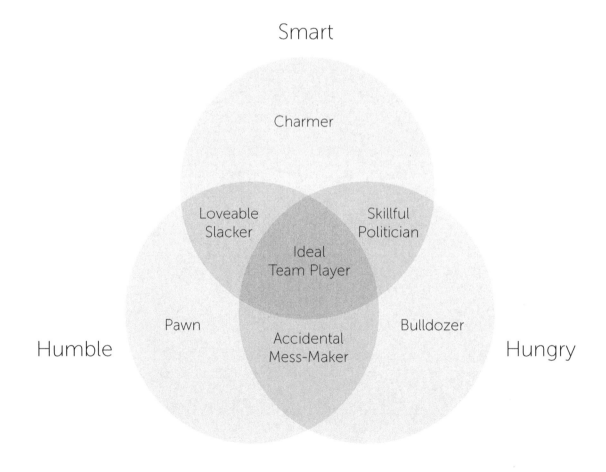

Smart

Charmer

Loveable Slacker

Skillful Politician

Ideal Team Player

Pawn

Bulldozer

Humble

Accidental Mess-Maker

Hungry

The Ideal Team Player © 2016 by Patrick Lencioni. All rights reserved.

SETTING THE SCENE

It was my first triathlon, and it was a short one. The swim was just one kilometre in a pool. I had signed up months before race day, and because swimming was my weakest discipline my guesstimate of my time was conservative.

Race day came, and the pool was cordoned off into thin lines. Each person would dive in and start swimming, and then there would be a ten-second countdown before the next person would do the same. Since guesstimating my time, I had done some more training, and the woman in front of me didn't look like she was going to be speedy.

The ten seconds counted down, I dived in, and before she'd reached the end of the first lane, I was right behind her. The etiquette in these scenarios is that if I wanted to overtake, I needed to tap her on the foot. It felt strange, but I gave her a couple of foot taps. But at the end of the next lap, she didn't let me overtake. She just started swimming the next lap.

I was now doing breaststroke behind her, and I again tapped her on the feet. But again, at the end of the pool she didn't stop. I began to get quite frustrated. *I'm quicker than you. Let me past!*

When she failed to stop for the third turn, I realised I only had one option. I needed to undertake. Like a stealth submarine I pushed off from the side, swimming underneath her and looking up through my goggles to make sure I was in front. But for some reason she sped up. I was now holding my breath, trying desperately to undertake her, and when I finally came to the surface, my breath was gone. I took a gulp of air too quickly and swallowed a huge mouthful of pool water.

Spluttering at the surface, trying not to look like I was drowning during a triathlon, I tried to get some composure and get my breath back. And as I did, she overtook me.

The one lesson learnt? Humility.

WHAT'S THE BIG IDEA?

Patrick Lencioni, author of *The Five Dysfunctions of a Team*, argues that much of what we do today relies upon teamwork. He believes good team players have three essential virtues: they are humble, hungry and smart.

All three of these attributes are necessary. If even one is missing in a co-worker, teamwork becomes much more difficult and sometimes even impossible. Let's unpack them.

Humble. Good team players are more concerned with the success of the team than their own credit and recognition. Humility does not mean that these team players don't acknowledge their skills and contributions, but they don't do so in a proud way. Humility is the greatest attribute for a team player. In contrast, arrogant team members, who seek attention and recognition, are dangerous to team dynamics.

Hungry. Good team players work hard. They are self-motivated and self-starters. They rarely have to be pushed and are often looking for more responsibility. They want to do the job well, but they are not workaholics. Work is not their entire identity.

Smart. Good team players are not necessarily intellectually smart, but they are emotionally intelligent. They understand people and can often read a room. They know how to listen and communicate. They may be described as kind, respectful and having good judgement.

These three characteristics create the ideal team player. When mapped on the Venn diagram above, we get an overlap, but we also get six more categories. We get Pawns, Bulldozers and Charmers, who only have one of the three characteristics. Then we get the following three categories where two of the characteristics overlap:

Accidental Mess-Maker. A Humble and Hungry team member may be able to achieve lots but will often leave a trail of relational problems in their wake.

Lovable Slackers. A Smart and Humble team member will often only do the bare minimum. They will need to be asked to work harder and can frustrate other team members.

Skilful Politician. A Hungry and Smart team member lacks humility and can cause real problems. They may know how to look humble, but behind the facade they are out to meet their own needs. By the time the team realises this, they may already have been manipulated.

THINKING BIBLICALLY

There is an array of (good and bad) examples of leadership in Scripture, but Jesus is our ultimate role model. He is Humble, Hungry and Smart!

In the ancient world, being Humble was not perceived to be a mark of a great leader, but the life of Jesus changed that. Most leadership gurus today identify humility as a core attribute of great leadership. Lencioni points directly to the example of Jesus in his book. Jesus' humility was characterised on a micro level in his actions, in the way he washed his disciples' feet and welcomed children. But it was also demonstrated on a macro level, in his willingness to take on human form and go to the cross (Philippians 2:5–8).

Jesus was also Hungry. This wasn't measured in the number of miracles or the size of the crowds but in obedience to the Father. Jesus was by no means a workaholic, as he regularly took time out to be with his Father, but when questioned about working on the sabbath, he responded, "'My Father is always at his work to this very day, and I too am working'" (John 5:17).

And finally, Jesus was Smart. He understood people. He saw their needs and was able to speak powerfully into situations. Having healed the woman who had been bleeding for twelve years, he called her out and affirmed her as 'Daughter' (Mark 5:34), identifying her need for more than physical healing. And when Pharisees came to him asking about whether it was right to pay taxes, he responded with the profound line: "'Give back to Caesar what is Caesar's, and to God what is God's'" (Mark 12:17).

When a bloodthirsty crowd set a trap for Jesus, having caught a woman in adultery, he skilfully defused the situation with the words, "'He who is without sin among you, let him throw a stone at her first'" (John 8:7 NKJV).

HOW DO I APPLY IT?

Managing a Team. With your team, talk through the three values, and then ask them to rank themselves in each of these areas. Ask each person to explain which is their lowest and why.

These values are not inherent and can be developed. Look for opportunities to help the team improve in these areas. This could be done by giving feedback, by encouraging the team to help coach one another and by celebrating these virtues corporately, sharing examples of people who have encapsulated all three.

Recruiting a Team. If great team players are Humble, Hungry and Smart, then you know what you are looking for when it comes to recruitment. It may be useful to think through your recruitment process to explore some creative ways to probe into the character of potential team players. This may involve asking specific questions around these three values, debriefing interviews with these values in mind and even doing some team exercises as part of the recruitment.

QUESTIONS FOR REFLECTION

How would you rank these three values in your life?

Is there a mentor that you could talk these through with, to help you intentionally cultivate them in your life?

How can you foster these virtues in those you lead?

GO FURTHER

Read *The Ideal Team Player* by Patrick Lencioni.[16]

Cultivating Critical Friends

KELLEY'S FIVE FOLLOWERSHIP STYLES
CHRIS

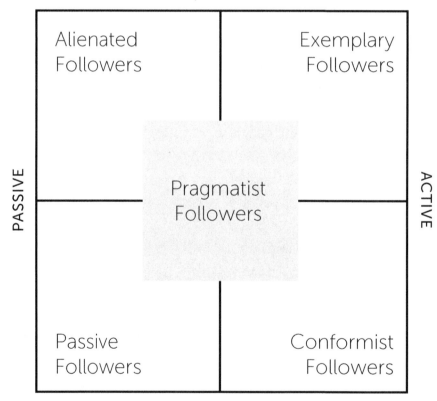

INDEPENDENT, CRITICAL THINKING

Alienated Followers	Exemplary Followers

PASSIVE · Pragmatist Followers · ACTIVE

Passive Followers	Conformist Followers

DEPENDENT, UNCRITICAL THINKING

SETTING THE SCENE

Leading around 75 per cent of the meetings I attend, I used to look forward to the 25 per cent I wasn't. I'll admit that I took them as an excuse to kick back a little and hit the cruise control. Perhaps I might subtly check a few messages on my phone, or in my head, slightly embarrassingly, try to work out who in the room would win in an arm wrestle. Virtual meetings were worse; I knew if I sat back from my screen enough, no one could see me reading and responding to emails, while I pretended to listen, not forgetting to piously nod at opportune moments. I didn't think I needed to bring my A-game to those meetings because someone else was ultimately responsible for directing them. I was just a follower.

Having been in employed church leadership for over a decade, I've attended dozens of inspiring leadership conferences, received weeks' worth of fascinating mentoring leadership sessions and read hundreds of leadership papers, but I cannot recall one instance of the topic of 'followership' being raised.

When I eventually did approach the topic, the Holy Spirit challenged me to be the critical friend that those I was following needed me and other followers to be. In the language of Dr Robert Kelley's bestselling book, *The Power of Followership*, I was a Passive Follower who had been challenged to be an Exemplary Follower.

WHAT'S THE BIG IDEA?

Leadership discourse has often suffered from its over-emphasis on leadership, forgetting that strong followership is essential for strong leadership. Much like a dance between two people, one cannot function well without the other.[17]

Kelley's matrix[18] plots followers according to Dependent Uncritical Thinking or Independent Critical Thinking on the y-axis and Passive Engagement or Active Engagement on the x-axis. The boxes plot five categories:

Passive Followers aren't actively participating or thinking critically; they let their leaders do all the heavy work.

Alienated Followers think critically and independently and don't participate in the groups they belong to.

Conformist Followers participate in their groups but are happy to just take orders.

Pragmatic Followers straddle both sides, being mediocrely active, and sometimes applying independent thinking and sometimes not.

Exemplary Followers are what every leader needs: actively engaged people bringing their best thinking to the table.

As a leader, the idea is to focus on creating a culture where you are surrounded by Exemplary Followers.

THINKING BIBLICALLY

Adidas's 2016 advertising campaign #NeverFollow[19] epitomised the culturally negative connotation of followership. But the Bible entreats us to follow Jesus (Mark 8:34), follow the State (Romans 13:1) and follow our local church leaders (Hebrews 13:17, 1 Corinthians 11:1, 1 Thessalonians 5:12). Therefore, we should be actively engaged in our followership roles.

In the Old Testament, Joseph is an excellent example of a great follower. First, he refuses to betray Pharaoh (Genesis 39:8–10). Then, despite being badly treated for his integrity (Genesis 39:19–20), when called upon, he not only interprets Pharaoh's dreams but also offers his critical thoughts as to how Pharaoh should respond (Genesis 41:25–36). This leaves Pharaoh to declare, "'Can we find anyone like this man, one in whom is the spirit of God?'" (verse 38), and elevate him into what was effectively the role of a prime minister (verses 40–41). In God's Kingdom, submission tends to precede elevation (Luke 14:8).

However, according to the Bible, being a good follower also means, when necessary, confronting leaders (2 Samuel 12, Galatians 2:11), refusing to obey leaders (Daniel 1:8, Esther 4:16) and even leaving leaders (Acts 15:36–41).

HOW DO I APPLY IT?

Like most leaders, you are probably a leader in some contexts and a follower in others. Indeed, it's unhealthy if you're leading in every context you're in. If you are, you may want to address that, for example by asking others to lead certain meetings even when you're there.

As a Follower. For the contexts in which you are a follower, plot yourself on Kelley's graph, reflect and then take appropriate action. For example, you may realise that you're being a Passive Follower in a team you volunteer for because you aren't motivated by the goals that the team are striving for, and so you may seek to clarify what the goals are in an effort to find meaning in them, or work out a way to volunteer elsewhere as a result.

As a Leader. Where you lead, you need to first ask the sobering question, 'Do I really want Exemplary Followers?', as it won't make for an easier life. If you're sure you do, then seek to diagnose Followership problems in your team. You may use your own intuition for this, or better, encourage team members to complete a readily available self-diagnostic tool,[20] with a follow-up chat. Use this process to identify where you are now, and where you want to get to. For example, you may want 90 per cent of your followers to honestly self-identify as Exemplary Followers within the next eighteen months.

You can then plan and implement the necessary change. For example, you may realise that you need to cultivate a more approachable style, critical to strengthening followers. Conversely, followers may recognise they need to take more responsibility for speaking up when not happy. Then you can seek to review the impact and sustain the improvements made.

QUESTIONS FOR REFLECTION

Where would you plot yourself on Kelley's graph as a follower? Why?

Where would you plot your followers on Kelley's graph? Why?

GO FURTHER

Read *The Power of Followership: How to Create Leaders People Want to Follow and Followers Who Lead Themselves* by Robert E. Kelley.

Watch 'Leadership and Followership: What Tango Teaches Us About These Roles in Life', youtube.com/watch?v=Cswrnc1dggg.

Changing Styles

THE SITUATIONAL LEADERSHIP MODEL

ANDY

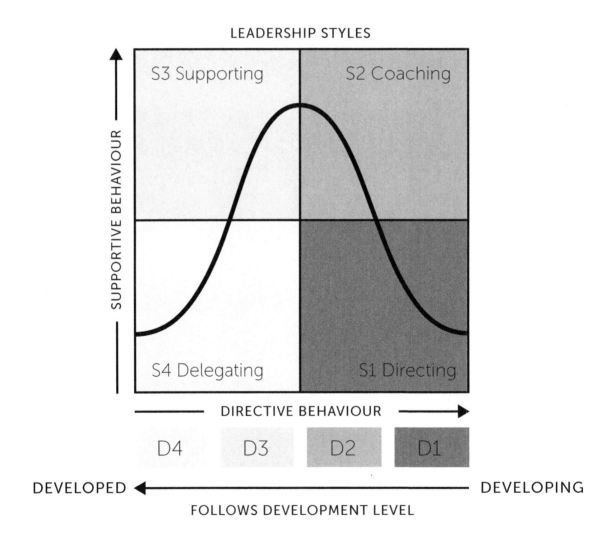

SETTING THE SCENE

It was our first fixture of the season, and I was captaining a new football team. Almost all the squad were eighteen-year-olds. They had wanted to join our club, so we had set up a new team for them.

Donning their new kit, there was a sense of expectation ahead of our first game as we gathered on the pitch. On the side-line I talked through the game plan. The defence were given their briefing, then the midfield and then the strikers, as we opted for a traditional 4-4-2 formation.

Things didn't go to plan.

Within fifteen minutes, we were 5-0 down, and by the end of the first half we were losing by double figures. It was a complete humiliation.

Each player had been delegated their role, but they were completely unprepared for a match on a full-size pitch, pitted against men in their 20s and 30s who knew how to use their physicality to manoeuvre our team off the ball.

The following week, I took the team to the park to go through eleven-a-side basics: where to stand when you're marking a corner, and how to move as a unit of players on a larger pitch.

In the different places we find ourselves leading teams, we need to understand who we are working with and what kind of leadership is needed.

WHAT'S THE BIG IDEA?

When it comes to leadership, we often have a picture of what a leader looks like in our mind. But the truth is that leadership looks different and varies enormously depending on the individual who is leading and the context they are leading in.

Situational leadership is simply about adapting the leadership style to the context in which you are operating. The theory originated with leadership expert Ken Blanchard and author Paul Hersey[21] who argued there was no one-size-fits-all leadership style. They created a framework for leaders to discern the best style of leadership for any given team according to their level of competence and commitment.

Their framework is set along two axes. The x-axis is Directive Behaviour – the amount of direction the leader gives an individual or team. The y-axis is Supportive Behaviour – the relational aspect of leadership, which includes the amount of dialogue, listening and encouraging that takes place with an individual or team. Both the Directing and Delegating styles involve low Supportive Behaviour but for different reasons. Directing is hands-on, with close supervision but limited opportunity for feedback, whereas Delegation is hands-off, and the team has authority to get on and achieve.

If we fail to recognise the need for different styles in different seasons and don't adjust accordingly, we can fail to get the best out of those we lead and fail to achieve set outcomes.

Blanchard and Hersey describe four leadership styles in their matrix:

Directing. Also known as guiding or telling, the leader tells people what to do and how to do it. This leadership style is useful when an individual or team requires close supervision. They may have little experience of commitment and need regular guidance. Your role as leader is to make the decisions and give clear direction.

Coaching. Also known as selling or persuading (as the leader gets buy-in for their ideas), this style involves a feedback loop between the leader and the team. This leadership style is helpful when there are team members who have some competence but need to develop in certain areas or when an individual is not particularly motivated. Using this approach, the leader will often help upskill individuals.

Supporting. Also known as participating or sharing, this style sees the leader being less directive as they empower the team to be more active in idea formation and decision making. This style of leadership is useful when an individual or team is becoming competent but lacks the confidence or motivation to do it entirely themselves. There is less direction from the leader but lots of support.

Delegating. Also known as empowering or monitoring, this style is hands-off leadership, whereby the team make most of the decisions and are largely responsible. This style of leadership works when a team are both highly competent and motivated. The leader must be willing to delegate authority, having set a clear vision with defined expectations.

As a leader, you will probably have a preferred style of leadership. Within an organisation or movement, there will also probably be a default leadership style.

Being a situational leader requires you to be flexible, aware of the shifting needs of the team and outcomes you hope to achieve. This requires active listening and clarifying of your aims. The team need to know that you, the leader, are trustworthy. It also requires an ability to encourage participation and the necessary coaching skills. Fundamentally, situational leaders need to stay in close communication with their team members.

Situational leadership is team focused and can help a leader get the most out of a team. However, it's important to note that it can have some negatives too. It can overly focus on short-term objectives, rather than the bigger picture, and can be burdensome for the leader. The lack of uniformity in leadership style can lead to team members feeling there's inconsistency, and they can find it hard to navigate the changing styles.

THINKING BIBLICALLY

Paul was a situational leader. We see this in his relationship with Timothy beginning in Acts 16. There's a phase of Directing as Paul tells Timothy he must be circumcised in order to avoid offending the religious Jews as Timothy travelled with Paul and Silas. Then, in Acts 17, Paul gets into trouble whilst preaching in Berea. Some of the Jews agitate the crowds, and Paul sees Timothy Coached and Supported by Silas as they are told to stay temporarily in Berea to nurture the young congregation that has been established.

Finally, there is Delegating. Paul trusts Timothy and sends him as his representative to the churches he was concerned about (1 Thessalonians 3:2; Philippians 2:19). While Paul is in prison, Timothy brings him updates, and several epistles mention that Paul sees Timothy as an equal. In the greetings to the church in Philippi, Paul writes, 'Paul and

Timothy, servants of Christ Jesus, to all God's holy people in Christ Jesus' (Philippians 1:1).

HOW DO I APPLY IT?

Those you lead directly. Which style of leadership do those you lead need in this season? (You may even want to share this model with your team and ask which situational leadership style works best for them.)

If they need Directing, are there ways to develop their skills with other, more experienced colleagues? For example, is there any peer-based learning that you could put in place?

If they need Coaching, how are you recognising their contributions and supporting their need to be developed?

If they need Supporting, how are you creating space for participation? Are you using the full potential of the skills and expertise of the team? How often do you use open-ended questions to help harness their ideas?

If they need Delegating, how are you empowering them? Have you given them the authority to move things forward without you and clarified the goals you want to reach?

Those you lead directly who lead others. Do these leaders feel constrained to a certain style of leadership? How could taking them through this model help them become more aware of their leadership styles?

QUESTIONS FOR REFLECTION

Thinking back upon your life, how have others demonstrated situational leadership to you? What can you learn from that?

What is your default style of leadership?

How can you adopt a situational leadership style?

GO FURTHER

Read *Management of Organizational Behavior* by Paul Hersey and Ken Blanchard.

Read the following blogs on situational leadership: blog.vantagecircle.com/contingency-leadership;

business-to-you.com/hersey-blanchard-situational-leadership-model.

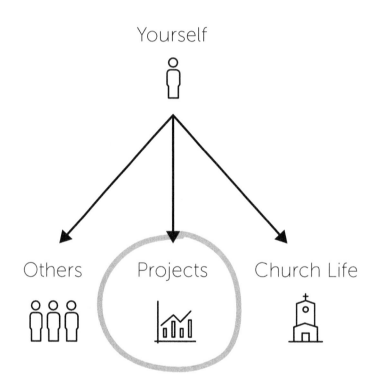

Yourself

Others   Projects   Church Life

LEADING PROJECTS

Having gained a tighter grip on leading yourself and others, you're hopefully champing at the bit to effect real change in whatever leadership position you are in. The need is never the call – that just leads to guilt – but we are called 'to do good works, which God prepared in advance for us to do' (Ephesians 2:10). These good works could be in the home or the workplace; either way, to use a military alliteration: Prior Planning Prevents Poor Performance. Therefore, the next thirteen diagrams drill down into the practical wisdom surrounding leading projects.

LEADING PROJECTS **INTERNALLY**:
Diagrams for Effective Internal Approaches

LEADING PROJECTS **EXTERNALLY**:
Diagrams for Effective External Approaches

LEADING PROJECTS **HOLISTICALLY**:
Diagrams for Effective Change

Meetings Matter

AXELROD'S MEETING CANOE

ANDY

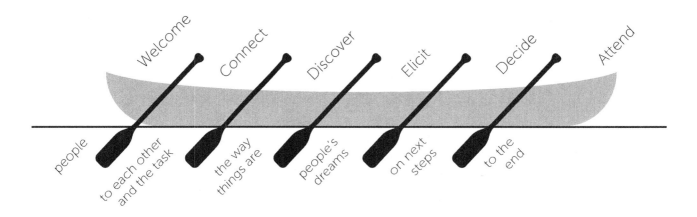

SETTING THE SCENE

I hate wasting time. When I am in a queue, I will keep looking at other lines to see how fast they are moving, and if a different one appears shorter, I'll jump lines.

One of the things that frustrates me more than anything is poorly run meetings. Over the years, I've experienced meetings that have no set agenda, meetings where the chair just likes the sound of his or her own voice, meetings which have overrun for hours, and meetings that have ended with less clarity, more confusion and no way forward.

Queen Victoria (who reigned from 1876 to 1901) wasn't too keen on meetings that wasted time either. One of her regular meetings was with the Privy Council, an advisory body to the British monarch made up of counsellors from senior political, judicial or ecclesiastical roles. She made it compulsory for everyone to remain standing during these meetings. The idea was to keep them short and to stop time being wasted!

This philosophy was adopted by Stelios Haji-Ioannou, the founder of EasyJet. Like Queen Victoria, he got so frustrated with time being wasted that he removed chairs from meetings.

It can be challenging to keep meetings on point and ensure they are a useful investment of everyone's time.

WHAT'S THE BIG IDEA?

The Meeting Canoe was developed by author and consulting firm co-founder Dick Axelrod as a framework to make meetings more effective.[1] The meeting outline consists of six important parts:

1. Welcome. From the outset, the environment for the meeting needs to be welcoming – valuing the people at the meeting and creating a space in which they feel safe to share. This begins before the meeting, as the agenda and venue are set, and continues from the initial greeting at the start all the way through to the meeting's conclusion.

2. Connect. Good meetings have space for connection. There needs to be an opportunity to build relationships between participants (which establishes trust) and between the participants and the task at hand (which creates energy).

3. Discover. Discover is about understanding where things are at. With different people in the meeting, there needs to be a shared picture of how things are. Rather than just give a presentation, invite each person to share their perspective, so there is a sense of discovery.

4. Elicit. Step four is about eliciting people's dreams. With trust and connection built into the first two steps, and an understanding of where things are at from step three, there is now space to imagine what could be. What is the shared dream?

5. Decide. Now you know where you are and where you want to be, the next step is about deciding what action will take place. In different situations, the decision-making process will come about in different ways. For example, it could be that the team makes a group decision or that the CEO, having listened to where things are at and the dreams people hold, decides what action is to take place.

6. Attend. Attending a meeting well is important. When people just gradually drift off, there can be misunderstandings on what was decided and who is responsible. Attending until the end is about reviewing decisions and clarifying next steps. People will leave with a sense of accomplishment.

THINKING BIBLICALLY

At the Council at Jerusalem (Acts 15) we get a glimpse into how the early church conducted their meetings. At this particular meeting, they were discussing the controversial issue of whether Gentiles needed to fulfil the Law of Moses once they accepted Christ. It's hard to fully extrapolate from the text, but when Paul and Silas met with the early church leaders, it looks like they followed a similar structure to Axelrod's canoe.

There was Welcome: 'When they came to Jerusalem, they were welcomed by the church and the apostles and elders' (Acts 15:4a).

There was a point to Connect: 'they reported everything God had done through them' (Acts 15:4b).

There was a process for them to Discover: 'Then some of the believers who belonged to the party of the Pharisees stood up and said, "The Gentiles must be circumcised and required to keep the law of Moses"' (Acts 15:5).

There was time for them to Elicit dreams: 'The apostles and elders met to consider this question' (Acts 15:6).

They had to Decide: '"It is my judgment, therefore, that we should not make it difficult for the Gentiles who are turning to God"' (Acts 15:19).

They chose to Attend until the end and make sure everyone knew what had been decided: 'With them they sent the following letter' (Acts 15:23).

HOW DO I APPLY IT?

As you work through the six sections of the Meeting Canoe, here are some suggestions for each step.

1. Welcome. Sending the agenda ahead of time gives people an opportunity to review it and think ahead. It's helpful to outline what you want to achieve and to ask them to feed back on the agenda with anything important they believe is missing. Is there more information they would like before the meeting to help them be better placed to make decisions? These protocols may require more thought and time beforehand, but they ensure that everyone feels valued and will help to make sure you all get the most out of the meeting.

2. Connect. If you are chairing the meeting, make space to Connect rather than diving straight into the agenda. Scan the room, make eye contact and check everyone is present. You might even want to ask or remind everyone briefly of why they are there and what they bring to the table.

3. Discover. We can think we have covered the Discover segment simply by preparing a paper for the meeting and regurgitating it, presuming everyone is on the same page. Asking people to share their reflections on what they have heard, and even what they disagree with, opens up a richer conversation of where things are at. Look for ways for people to share their unique perspectives.

4. Elicit. For this step, help people dream for the future, using open-ended questions, such as: What could this look like in five years' time? What do we expect the impact of this task to be? What does success look like?

5. Decision. To make sure this stage is covered, it may help to articulate the decisions that need to be made in the agenda. Sharing those questions in written form (a screen, whiteboard or printout), can help to focus the conversation and ensure progress has been made. In the minutes, it is vital that the decisions made are articulated and the reasoning behind them is clearly noted.

6. Attend. It can be helpful to recap all the decisions that have been made in the meeting alongside who is responsible and their timeline for action. As you do this, give people an opportunity to feed back there and then if they think there have been any mistakes in the recording.

QUESTIONS FOR REFLECTION

What have been the best meetings you have attended? Why did they run so well?

Look through a recent meeting agenda. What could you have done differently?

Which of the elements of Axelrod's Meeting Canoe are you weakest and strongest in? Is there someone who could help you sharpen future meetings?

GO FURTHER

See more at axelrodgroup.com.

Intentionally Connecting

THE COMMUNICATION STRATEGY CONTINUUM

CHRIS

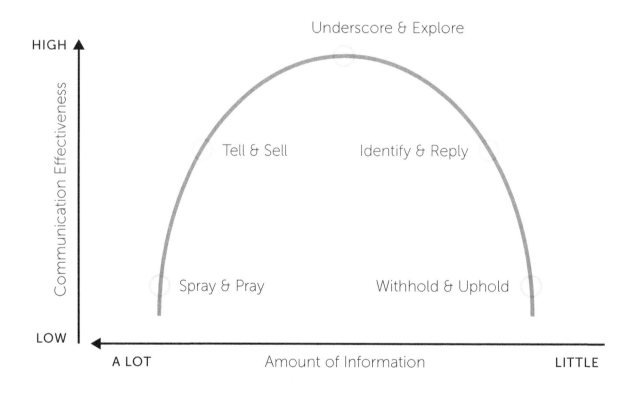

SETTING THE SCENE

One of the greatest communication errors in modern history was the British implementation of the Revenue Act in 1767. Following the Seven Years' War (1756–1763), where Britain and France fought for global dominance, Britain was strapped for cash. Britain's solution was to rush through, without consultation, a tax on the huge tea market on their American colonists.

The Americans were understandably unhappy, crying, 'No taxation without representation' – believing taxes shouldn't be imposed upon them when they didn't have a say. They responded by boycotting tea imported from Britain. Things escalated, resulting in British tax enforcers killing several American protestors in Boston, eventually leading to the raid known as the Boston Tea Party.

On 16 December 1773, colonists disguised as Native Americans famously emptied chests of British tea into Boston harbour. The crisis continued to escalate, culminating in the American Revolutionary War, which began near Boston in 1775. A long and bloody conflict eventually resulted in America securing independence from Britain in 1783. A seemingly small decision to tax tea had a ripple effect that is still felt today.

In the words of Dr Phillip Clampitt, bestselling author of *Communicating for Managerial Effectiveness*, Britain's communication approach had been to 'Withhold and Uphold'.[2]

WHAT'S THE BIG IDEA?

When leading internally, you can 'communicate about anything', but you can't 'communicate about everything'.[3] Choices are made, consciously or unconsciously, about what, how, when and where you communicate to those you work with. Clampitt encourages leaders to think more strategically about their approach, no matter the size of their organisation. He identified five common approaches to internal communication, plotted on the graph according to their effectiveness and the amount of information contained within them.

Spray & Pray. Leaders shower employees with all kinds of information in the hope employees will be able to sort out the significant from insignificant. The assumption is that more information equals better communication. Simple, yes. Effective, rarely.

Tell & Sell. Leaders communicate a more limited set of messages, believing that these address core organisational issues. First, they tell employees about the key issues. Second, they sell employees the wisdom of their approach. This approach lacks meaningful dialogue, assuming employees are passive information receivers, and often leads to long-term scepticism, if not cynicism.

Underscore & Explore. This is consistently the most effective approach, where leaders focus on several fundamental issues most clearly linked to organisational success, while allowing employees the creative freedom to explore the implications of those ideas in a disciplined way. This approach creatively synthesises leaders' initiatives and employees' concerns.

Identify & Reply. Leaders focus on employees' concerns, identifying key issues and responding to these. This is problematic, as the leader allows employees to completely set the agenda, rather than focusing on the organisation's objectives.

Withhold & Uphold. Leaders withhold information until it is deemed necessary to divulge. Secrecy and control are often the implicit values here, with the assumption that information is power, and the leader consequently refraining from sharing.

THINKING BIBLICALLY

When we communicate well with those we partner with, we are imitating God himself. Hebrews 1:1–2a, says, 'In the past God spoke to our ancestors through the prophets at many times and in various ways, but in these last days he has spoken to us by his Son …'.

The prophets in the Old Testament show us the persistent and underlying key issues that are laid upon God's heart, such as his holiness and desire for our loyalty, or his care for the suffering and our need to respond in love. Yet he also appointed priests and created the sacrificial system, so that communication would always be two-way.

Then God went further, not even withholding his perfect word, Jesus (John 1:1, Romans 8:32). His death and resurrection now mean we have a perfect mediator (1 Timothy 2:5), with whom and through whom we can communicate.

Of course, Jesus now continues to communicate through his creation, his Spirit, his Word, and his church.

HOW DO I APPLY IT?

You likely already have communication tools, such as a weekly bulletin, a regular staff meeting or one-to-ones. The key is to think about the main points, both now and in the future, that you need to communicate and appropriately hear back on. Then ask if the tools you have are fit for purpose, and adjust accordingly.

For example, you may realise that far too much information is going out in your weekly bulletin with no response mechanism, so you decide to significantly cut the amount of content and create response channels, such as posting on social media channels where comments can be made. Alternatively, you may realise your staff meetings have become a free-for-all, where the direction is led by everyone's opinion, and so you introduce a more rigid agenda with allocated timings, still allowing for feedback but in a more controlled manner. Or you may recognise that at one-to-ones, you don't really allow the other person to clarify or critique decisions you have made, so you endeavour to ask more questions, leaving space for them to respond.

QUESTIONS FOR REFLECTION

Have you ever worked at an organisation where you felt really committed to the vision?

What about their internal communication was effective?

Where would you plot your usual internal communication approach on the Communication Strategy Continuum?

GO FURTHER

Read *A Strategy for Communicating about Uncertainty* by Phillip Clampitt, Robert DeKoch and Thomas Cashman.

What Matters?

EISENHOWER'S PRIORITY MATRIX

ANDY

	URGENT	NOT URGENT
IMPORTANT	Do it now	Schedule a time for it
NOT IMPORTANT	Who can do it for you?	Eliminate it

SETTING THE SCENE

When I played the opening sequence of the 2009 Disney-Pixar film *Up* in a church service, there wasn't a dry eye in the room.

A phenomenal piece of storytelling, the clip beautifully tells the story of Carl, who falls in love and then marries his childhood sweetheart, Ellie. The sequence moves through the decades of their life together as they watch clouds, read, renovate their home and try for a family.

When Ellie suffers a miscarriage, and they discover they can't have children, Carl reminds Ellie of her childhood dreams by bringing his wife her childhood scrapbook. The idea of adventure consoles her, and as a couple they begin to save money in a jar for a dream trip to Paradise Falls.

However, time after time, pressing needs – such as money to fix a car tyre, a medical bill for a broken leg and house repairs – see them open the jar early to spend their savings on their urgent needs. Finally, the sequence ends with Ellie's death. And in the same church in which they got married, they hold her funeral. Grief-stricken, Carl heads home, and the screen fades to black. They never got to take the trip.

We can all relate to the sadness of having a dream that we never quite get around to.

WHAT'S THE BIG IDEA?

The Eisenhower Matrix has its origins in a speech delivered by President Eisenhower in 1954, in which he explained, 'I have two kinds of problems: the urgent and the important. The urgent are not important, and the important are never urgent.'[4]

Repackaged by Stephen Covey in his best-selling book, *The 7 Habits of Highly Effective People*,[5] the matrix has two axes, one for Urgent and one for Important. The tool helps us discern where best to focus in order not to be merely productive but effective, so that we don't miss out on the important things because we have been too focused on the urgent.

Too often we spend all our energy firefighting and focusing on urgent tasks at the expense of the less urgent tasks that are far more important. Using the matrix, we can put all of our tasks (both personal and work) into one of four quadrants:

Urgent and Important: Tasks that need to be done as a priority. These tasks have tight deadlines, and there'll often be consequences for not taking immediate action. Tasks in this quadrant can include unexpected things (such as a data hack, a leak in the roof or a sick child), or tasks that have been put off that are now urgent.

Not Urgent and Important: Tasks that need to be scheduled. These tasks are normally related to your longer-term aspirations. There may not be a set deadline, and so it is easy to keep putting them at the bottom of the list. Tasks in this quadrant might include things like regular personal fitness, forecasting longer-term budgets or team away-days. These tasks are not about responding to problems but about growth and development. The more we focus our time in this quadrant, the more we take pressure from future problems in the Urgent and Important quadrant.

Urgent and Not Important: Tasks that we are expected to do. These tasks don't normally fit with our longer-term goals and are often about responding to what others want from us. Tasks may include meetings we feel we should attend or responding to alerts on our phones. Perhaps one of the most common is responding to emails promptly. Living in this quadrant can make you feel you aren't in control of your diary. It requires us to understand that responding to the Urgent and Not Important impacts our effectiveness. We may need to be clearer with those asking for help on what we can offer, changing some of our working habits (for example, switching off notifications), or saying no more regularly. Tasks in this quadrant may also be able to be delegated or outsourced. For example, on a personal level, you might choose to order your weekly shopping with a supermarket that offers delivery.

Not Urgent and Not Important: Tasks that are wasting your time. We all need some downtime, but tasks in this quadrant are distractions that leave you unfulfilled. Tasks may include things like finishing the boxset you are not even enjoying or scrolling through social media.

THINKING BIBLICALLY

One of the big challenges with the Eisenhower Matrix is how we discern what is Urgent and what is Important. We can easily be led by our emotions or by our selfish desires. Knowing who we are and what we are called to do is important. Jesus was often interrupted (for example, by people wanting healing or wanting to challenge him). He often saw those interruptions as Urgent and Important, even though they may not have been scheduled in his diary.

What is clear from the life of Jesus is that he spent time in prayer. That can seem Not Urgent and Important, but it is foundational. In Matthew 6:33, Jesus says, 'But seek first the kingdom of God and His righteousness' (ESV).

HOW DO I APPLY IT?

You can do this exercise for yourself or with your team members. The big question you want to ask is: Which quadrant is most time being spent in? The aim is to be spending more time in what's classified as Not Urgent and Important.

Spend a week noting down all the activities you do and how long you spend doing them. (You might do this for work or for home activities or for both.) For example: answering emails (45 mins), organising house insurance (20 mins), writing a blog post (40 mins).

Once you have collected a week's data, organise your tasks into the four quadrants. You do this by simply asking: Was this Urgent for me? Was this Important to me?

The answer to these questions is dictated by your desired outcomes.

Having sorted the tasks into piles, tot up how much time was spent in each quadrant. Then ask yourself this: Are you satisfied with how you are spending your time? If the answer is no, then consider whether any of the outcomes below fit your profile.

TOO MUCH TIME IN URGENT AND IMPORTANT

Invest more time in planning to prevent problems. Look at your diary for the month ahead and schedule time based on what you want to achieve. If lots of what you are doing is coming from external sources, you may need to talk with colleagues or clients about how to address this.

TOO MUCH TIME IN URGENT AND NOT IMPORTANT

Write out specific tasks that regularly appear, and devise steps on how to tackle them. For example, if you have regular emails to respond to, can you set aside certain times to attend to them and put on your out-of-office at other times? If you are regularly interrupted, is there a new working rhythm that might help prevent interruptions?

TOO MUCH TIME IN NOT URGENT AND NOT IMPORTANT

Identify the biggest drains on your time and explore healthier habits. For example, rather than scrolling on social media, go for a short, brisk walk.

QUESTIONS FOR REFLECTION

Which quadrant do you naturally operate in?

If you were to ask family or co-workers, would they give the same answer?

Do you struggle to distinguish between what is important and not important? Who could help you with this?

What could your diary look like going forward? Do you need to schedule in time with God?

GO FURTHER

See eisenhower.me/eisenhower-matrix for more.

Thinking Speeds

KAHNEMAN'S SYSTEM 1 AND 2 THINKING

CHRIS

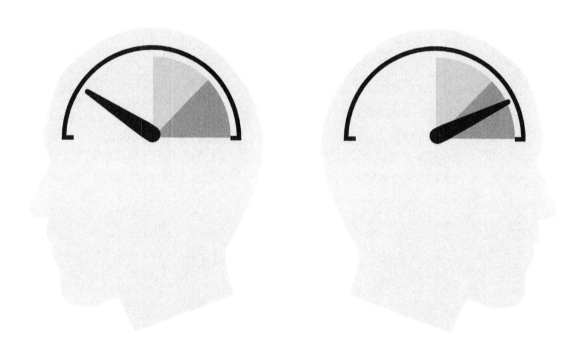

SETTING THE SCENE

Aesop is the ancient Greek slave and storyteller credited with writing the well-known fable 'The Tortoise and the Hare'. His original, translated into English, goes as follows:

A Hare was making fun of the Tortoise one day for being so slow. 'Do you ever get anywhere?' he asked with a mocking laugh. 'Yes,' replied the Tortoise, 'and I get there sooner than you think. I'll run you a race and prove it.'

The Hare was much amused at the idea of running a race with the Tortoise, but for the fun of the thing he agreed. So the Fox, who had consented to act as judge, marked the distance and started the runners off. The Hare was soon far out of sight, and to make the Tortoise feel very deeply how ridiculous it was for him to try a race with a Hare, he lay down beside the course to take a nap until the Tortoise should catch up.

The Tortoise meanwhile kept going slowly but steadily, and, after a time, passed the place where the Hare was sleeping. But the Hare slept on very peacefully; and when at last he did wake up, the Tortoise was near the goal. The Hare now ran his swiftest, but he could not overtake the Tortoise in time. The race is not always to the swift.[6]

Many moral lessons have been extracted from this story over the centuries, but here 'The Tortoise and the Hare' serves as a metaphor for two approaches we can take towards thinking. The Hare represents our fast, impulsive and often overconfident thinking, and the Tortoise represents our slower, more reflective and often more successful thinking. Or, to put it in the language of psychologist Daniel Kahneman, they could represent System 1 and System 2 thinking.

WHAT'S THE BIG IDEA?

System 1 and 2 thinking are labels popularised by Kahneman's bestselling book *Thinking, Fast and Slow*.[7] System 1 thinking 'operates automatically and quickly, with little or no effort and no sense of voluntary control'.[8] It is this thinking that acts like an autopilot in everyday life, enabling us to make thousands of daily decisions, with little attention needed, such as walking or basic conversation.

System 2 thinking, however, 'allocates attention to the effortful mental activities that demand it'.[9] We use this thinking whenever a level of focus is required to complete a task, such as a complex maths equation or exploring the implications of diagrams!

Neither system is perfect; both have strengths and weaknesses, and sometimes one is more appropriate for a situation than another. There are moments when confident and fast, Hare-like thinking is appropriate, such as for urgent and non-important decisions. There are moments when slow and considered, Tortoise-like thinking is appropriate, such as for non-urgent, important decisions.

The challenge comes in applying the correct system appropriately. The aim is both to prevent rash decisions, in which the consequences of sloppy thinking are reaped, and to avoid paralysis from analysis, in which ultimately nothing is accomplished.

THINKING BIBLICALLY

Have you ever sat through a court case? As an ex-court chaplain, I have to admit that my opinion on whether someone was guilty or not usually depended on whether I was listening to the prosecution or defence lawyer at the time. I was glad to realise I wasn't alone in this when I stumbled across Proverbs 18:17: 'In a lawsuit the first to speak seems right, until someone comes forward and cross-examines.'

I think this proverb highlights that what's true in the court-room is true of much of life: we often make rash judge-ments and therefore rash decisions. Proverbs speaks again and again of being careful to think correctly, perhaps most memorably in the famous verse, 'Trust in the LORD with all of your heart and do not lean on your own understand-ing. In all your ways acknowledge him, and he will make straight your paths' (Proverbs 3:5–6 ESV).

In order to not rely on our own understanding, three biblical steps are necessary.

First, recognise that your own understanding is flawed. Just as overconfidently jumping on to an unstable chair can cause embarrassment, so can being overconfident in our knowledge. Agur, one of the authors of Proverbs, hyperbolises a preferred approach in chapter 30:2–3: 'Surely I am only a brute, not a man; I do not have human understanding. I have not learned wisdom, nor have I attained to the knowledge of the Holy One.' The funny thing is, Agur goes on to share mic-dropping wisdom. It turns out wisdom entails being humble about how much we know and understand. If you're not convinced, remember that it was intelligent, well-read, religious people who thought they were doing God a favour when they got Jesus killed.

Second, test your thinking. Although you may not like the term 'Devil's advocate', it can be a helpful approach for questioning a decision. It originates from 'advocatus diaboli' (Latin for 'Devil's advocate'), which was a former official position within the Catholic Church. It was their role to argue against the canonisation of a candidate, to ensure only the right people were made saints. Proverbs 21:5 sums it up like this: 'The plans of the diligent lead surely to advantage, But everyone who is hasty comes surely to poverty' (NASB1995).

Third, get good counsel. The Spiritual Growth Network diagram (see page 48) is useful here to ensure you surround yourself with helpful people. It's important not to sell ideas to your counsel for their approval, but to share with the hope of helpful scrutiny. Proverbs 11:14 says, 'Where there is no guidance the people fall, But in abundance of coun-selors there is victory' (NASB1995), and Proverbs 12:15 says, 'The way of fools seems right to them, but the wise listen to advice'.

HOW DO I APPLY IT?

Kahneman's hope was to give us a vocabulary for evaluating our own and others' thinking.[10] The next time you need to make a decision, try speaking out loud, 'Does this decision need System 1 or System 2 thinking?' If it's System 2, you'll need to stop other activities and really give it some thought.

It is important to be aware of our implicit biases, particularly within our System 1 thinking. For example:

The Status Quo Bias. We tend to want to keep things the way they are.

The Halo Bias. We tend to think that if something or someone is good, everything they do or are is good.

The Ikea Bias. We tend to be irrationally attached to items that we have personally created.[11]

Being aware of these kinds of biases can help you to transition to System 2 thinking and avoid making big mistakes.

QUESTIONS FOR REFLECTION

Try this exercise. In your head, work out how many seconds there are in six months. How does this example help you to recognise the need to slow down and apply System 2 thinking to answer more complex problems?

What is a bad decision you have made? Could applying System 2 thinking have helped?

Do you suffer from paralysis from analysis? Why?

GO FURTHER

Read *Thinking, Fast and Slow* by Daniel Kahneman.

Communicating Change

THE A TO B LINE

CHRIS

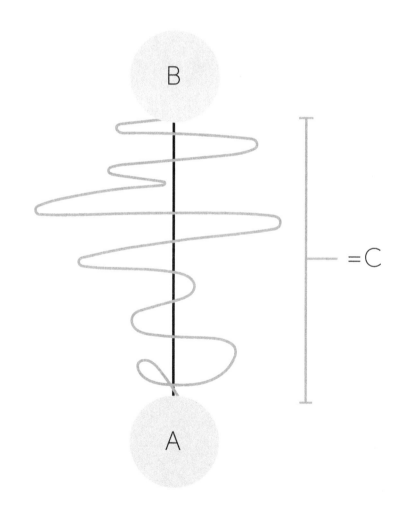

SETTING THE SCENE

My good friend Anjelo had one of the toughest starts in life. Growing up in northern Uganda during the '80s and '90s, his land and people were devastated by the Lord's Resistance Army, led by Joseph Kony. Anjelo was left fatherless and penniless, unable to afford the schooling that could lift him and his family out of poverty.

But Anjelo, hearing the gospel and coming to faith, decided to pray. One night, following an intense time of prayer, he had a vision of Jesus opening up doors for schooling, with the promise that God would provide him with education until he grew tired of studying.

A rare and unexpected World Vision sponsorship to attend school soon followed. Excelling at school, he then gained an even rarer government sponsorship to attend university. Gaining employment at the Bank of Uganda, he soon went on to be awarded a prestigious World Bank sponsorship to complete an economics doctorate at the University of Leeds. Now, understandably, he's a bit tired of studying!

When we met, and bonded over our love of football, Anjelo burned with a new vision to pass on the blessing he had received to others. In October 2021 I was privileged to support him with the launching of The Safe Haven Academy. Built in Anjelo's home village, the academy now welcomes over two hundred students and provides quality education to many who could not otherwise access or afford it.

God-breathed visions are incredibly powerful, bringing life, blessing and hope.

WHAT'S THE BIG IDEA?

A lot of leadership is about effecting change; using your influence to take a situation from point A to point B. Communicating a vision for that journey is absolutely critical, because it doesn't matter how good your change strategy is, if the communication of the vision is poor, it will likely fail.

The diagram points out three critical communication points for any vision:

Point A. This is the status quo, where things are at the moment. It's your job to communicate why this is not an okay place to be. Further, why is this not an okay place to be for any significant length of time? You need to create a sense of urgency, using something that connects with the heart and not just the head, best done through 'verbal pictures that are worth a thousand words'.[12] For example, you may share personal stories of the struggles people face to explain why a current situation is no longer fit for purpose.

Point B. This is where you want to get to, where things could be. It's your job to communicate what this place will look and feel like, as well as outlining simply, but not simplistically, some of the necessary steps it will take to get there. A critical point here is to link this vision to your 'superordinate', or overarching goal.[13] For example, if you're leading an overtly Christian organisation, you might link it to how it fulfils your vision statement, the Great Commission (Matthew 28:16–20) or the Great Commandment (Matthew 22: 37–38).

Area C. Here lies the erratic journey line that represents how implementing vision often goes, in juxtaposition to the straight line of how we plan the journey. Even the most carefully outlined strategies need adjustment along the way, as unforeseen challenges, setbacks or opportunities raise their heads. Point B itself might eventually look a lot different to how you first visualised it.

Therefore, at different points in Area C, it's important to communicate openly and inform people of the real challenges you are facing; otherwise, they may fill the communication gap and put their own misinformed spin on it. Points A and B also need continual reiteration, to remind people why you're persisting with this goal.

THINKING BIBLICALLY

The go-to biblical story for seeing a vision become reality is found in Nehemiah.

It's around 600 BC and the people of God have been exiled from their land. At the end of 2 Chronicles, the Holy Spirit presses Cyrus, the king of Persia, to allow the Jews to go back to Jerusalem and rebuild the temple. The book of Ezra details this rebuilding, and a spiritual renewal follows. However, there's a major problem (Point A): There are no walls.

This gets under Nehemiah's skin, but before arrogantly communicating a vision for change, he first humbly undertakes a prolonged season of prayer (Nehemiah 1:4).

Eventually, the vision communication point comes, where he paints a strong picture of Points A and B: 'Then I said to them, "You see the trouble we are in: Jerusalem lies in ruins, and its gates have been burned with fire. Come, let us rebuild the wall of Jerusalem, and we will no longer be in disgrace"' (Nehemiah 2:17).

He also informs people why, after 150 years of the walls being like this, something should be done: 'I also told them about the gracious hand of my God on me and what the king had said to me' (Nehemiah 2:18a). No wonder, then, 'They replied, "Let us start rebuilding." So they began this good work' (Nehemiah 2:18b).

The rest of Nehemiah unpacks the significant obstacles to implementing, and then later sustaining, a vision (Area C). But Nehemiah takes opposition as a sign to continue with God's vision rather than a sign to stop. In just fifty-two days, Nehemiah and his team reinstated an estimated 2.5-mile wall, 40 feet tall and 20 feet thick, consisting of around 1.5 billion tonnes of material. No wonder onlookers 'realised that this work had been done with the help of [their] God' (Nehemiah 6:16).[14]

HOW DO I APPLY IT?

The critical question to work through is: What vision am I going to communicate, to whom, when and how? The 'when', or timing, of vision communication is especially significant, ensuring it takes place in the right macro and micro moment for the organisation. For example, if you're a church leader, on the macro scale you may want to use The Life Cycle and Stages of Congregational Development (see page 202) to determine whether a new vision is right for your church at the moment. Or on the micro scale, you may delay communicating a new vision until the busy Christmas season has finished.

It is also critical that vision communication is shared within the right culture. Management consultant Peter Drucker is attributed with the saying, 'Culture eats strategy for breakfast.' Indeed, if a strategy for a new vision is to grow, it needs to be planted in the right cultural soil. Therefore, before seeking to initiate a new vision, it is incumbent to first ask whether the organisation's culture is ready for it.

QUESTIONS FOR REFLECTION

What's the greatest vision communication you've ever heard? Why?

What story could you use to communicate a vision you're running with at the moment?

What visions have hit stumbling blocks in your organisation? What communication could you implement surrounding them?

GO FURTHER

Read John P. Kotter, 'Accelerate: Building Strategic Agility for a Faster-Moving World' in *Harvard Business Review*.[15]

Developing Relationships

THE COMMUNICATION TRIANGLE

ANDY

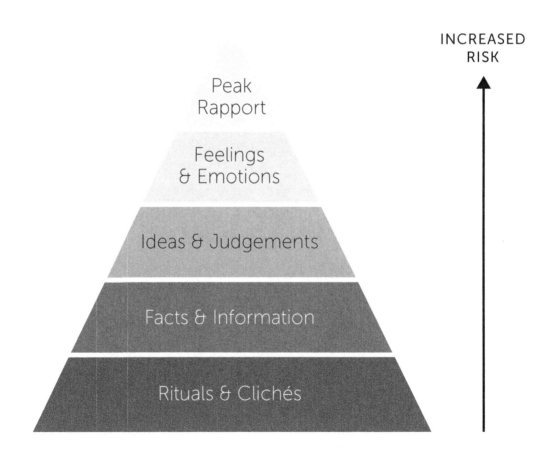

INCREASED
RISK

Peak
Rapport

Feelings
& Emotions

Ideas & Judgements

Facts & Information

Rituals & Clichés

SETTING THE SCENE

The average person will interact with ten thousand people in their lifetime.

Many of those interactions will be on a superficial level. I'm aware of that in my own life. There are some people I see regularly – whether that be outside the school gate or in the pub or even at church – and the conversations always revolve around the latest football scores, the cost of a pint these days or the length of the sermon. Although I know things about these people, I don't feel I *know* them.

I have also had interactions where the conversation has become deep too quickly. Awkwardly so. Before I was married, I once met a woman who, on the second time of chatting with her, downloaded her whole life story in one sitting. It felt like I was assuming the role of her therapist rather than starting a journey of friendship.

I have also experienced some interactions that began with pleasantries and have gradually become deep friendships. I think about some of the dads of my kids' friends. We began solely talking about our children – the school runs, teachers and after school clubs – but have gradually learnt about one another and become true friends.

We all experience some interactions that lead to acquaintances and some acquaintances that become good friends.

WHAT'S THE BIG IDEA?

The Communications Triangle describes levels of human interaction. It moves from Rituals and Clichés, which are very safe, all the way through to riskier interactions, where we reveal more of who we are and form deeper relationships or Peak Rapport.

This communication diagram originated from psychologist Richard Francisco, who mapped out five levels that represent increasing degrees of risk and learning in our interactions with one another.[16]

Rituals and Clichés. This includes the most basic of interactions that we have with multiple people almost every day, as we pass a neighbour or exchange pleasantries with a shopkeeper. We acknowledge each other. The interaction is polite and often involves hellos and goodbyes. There may be little eye contact or listening taking place as we operate almost on autopilot, perhaps talking about the weather! These interactions are formulaic, but they are valuable as they give us a sense of security and can become building blocks for deepening relationships.

Facts and Information. The next level involves some listening but is still superficial. The participants are still acquaintances. They report the facts and information through statements that are safe and have little emotion. These kinds of conversations can happen when we keep meeting the same parent at the school gate, and we go beyond the initial pleasantries. This is still small talk, as the topics are safe; we are careful not to overstep in our assumptions, overshare or ask something too personal.

Ideas and Judgements. The dividing line between this level and Facts and Information can be difficult to specify. At this level, we think more proactively as we share opinions and interpret facts and information. We may hear things we agree with and disagree with. Many of our professional relationships operate at this level. We may well have feelings as we are communicating, but we do not talk about them, which can sometimes be why a working situation breaks down.

Feelings and Emotions. In the fourth level we display how we feel not only through our words but also through tone and body language. At this stage, we are more comfortable being ourselves. There is honesty, but sometimes sharing how we feel can be challenging.

Peak Rapport. This represents the pinnacle of the Communication Triangle. Conversations now involve how we feel about one another. These conversations are authentic, and there is space to be vulnerable. We have less experience with these types of conversations, and so they can seem daunting, but when we interact on this level we learn much more about each other and develop a depth of empathy.

Each of these levels is important and serves a purpose. When you are working with people on a project, the key thing is to understand what level you are connecting on and to be able to build trust to move to a level of relationship that will help you work effectively together. If you try to go too deep too quickly, you can undermine the relationship.

THINKING BIBLICALLY

When we look at Jesus' relationship with his disciples, we see some dramatic highs and lows as they journey together. They walked, ate, ministered and took boat journeys together.

With this as a backdrop, Jesus asks, 'Who do you say I am?' (Matthew 16:15) and Peter answers, 'You are the Messiah, the Son of the living God' (verse 16).

In Jesus' words, there is honesty and vulnerability as he affirms his identity, telling them not to tell others. Jesus then speaks over Peter's life about his calling.

Next, Jesus begins to speak about his death, and at this point, Peter takes him to one side and rebukes him, 'Never, Lord!' (verse 22).

Jesus' response?

'Get behind me, Satan! You are a stumbling block to me; you do not have in mind the concerns of God, but merely human concerns' (verse 23).

There is no messing around. No superficial pleasantries. This conversation is raw, real and honest. Jesus and Peter have deep concern for one another and are able to speak truth openly.

Truly 'knowing' one another – seeing who God has made us to be, sharing vulnerably about our true identities, and affirming one another in who we are and what we're called to live out, happens when there is Peak Rapport.

HOW DO I APPLY IT?

In the various projects we're engaged with, we will be working with all sorts of people, which will require varying levels of interaction. At all these levels the ability to build rapport is important. Rapport helps to reduce underlying tensions and get the best out of everyone. With some people it feels easy to build rapport, but with others it can be hard to get past facts and information. Here are some helpful questions to think through:

- At what level do you communicate with the different people you work with? Do you avoid deeper conversations?
- How might we create more space for deepening connections with those we work with? Do we need to make space outside of meetings so that we can connect more with certain people we're working with?
- What might we do to develop trust with others?

QUESTIONS FOR REFLECTION

How good am I at building rapport with people?

Do I generally hold back on sharing emotions, or am I more likely to overshare?

What kind of communication is appropriate for the different people I lead?

Do we sometimes rush deeper conversations without the necessary levels of trust?

GO FURTHER

Read *Why Am I Afraid to Tell You Who I Am?* by John Powell.[17]

Future Proofing

THE SCENARIO FRAMEWORK
CHRIS

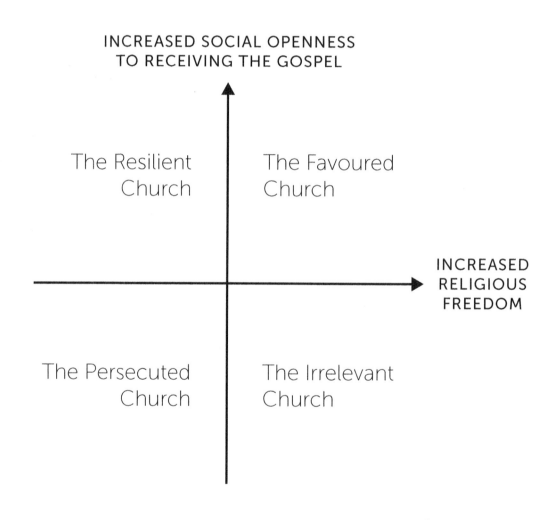

INCREASED SOCIAL OPENNESS
TO RECEIVING THE GOSPEL

The Resilient
Church

The Favoured
Church

INCREASED
RELIGIOUS
FREEDOM

The Persecuted
Church

The Irrelevant
Church

SETTING THE SCENE

Before becoming a church pastor, I worked in TV production. The best show I worked on was *100 Greatest War Movies,* where I literally got paid to watch war films. The toughest show I worked on was about predictions that had failed. Convincing guests who'd made an erroneous prediction to appear on TV was repeatedly tricky!

For instance, I wasn't shocked that former Liverpool footballer Alan Hansen didn't reply to a request to talk about the infamous 'You can't win anything with kids' prediction, a comment he made on *Match of the Day* in 1995 about the young Manchester United squad. Under Sir Alex Ferguson, the club went on to win the cup double that season and the infamous cup treble in 1999.

I expected yet another interview rejection when I phoned a senior advisor to British Prime Minister Tony Blair, so I was near speechless when, after diplomatically outlining the premise of the programme, the advisor agreed to be on the show. As a professional futurist, he was confident in his historic success and said something to the effect of, 'As long as I'm getting some serious predictions right, I'm bringing value.' And so he gave a humble and insightful interview for our number one terrible prediction: the impact of the millennium bug.

Seeking to predict the future is fraught with difficulties and dangers. However, considering possible future scenarios, and how your organisation might prepare for them now, is no bad thing.

WHAT'S THE BIG IDEA?

Only God knows the future, but with careful thought, it's possible to create some potential scenarios of what the future world may look like. Bearing this in mind, you can then consider what actions you may take to future proof your project or organisation as much as possible. Scenario planning is both a science and an art form that has evolved in an attempt to help that process. Here is a simplified five-step process, using a working example from the diagram:

1. Work out a central question. What is the future scenario you are considering? You need to define the parameters of the scenario you will plot onto the diagram, which relates to a time in the not-too-distant future.

For our working example in the diagram, we are considering the question: What is the context for the church in the West in fifteen years? Other scenario examples might be: What could our coffee business's supply chain look like in ten years, or, for our charity supporting asylum seekers, what might the refugee context be in five years?

2. Identify two driving forces. These are potentially significant future changes which would have a high level of impact on your central question.

A PESTEL analysis can be helpful here. Consider what relevant issues arise in the different strategic spheres: Political, Economic, Social, Technological, Environmental and Legal. Ascertain two key issues that have the greatest impact on your central question. For example, global trade co-operation and consumer behaviour in relation to climate change may have a significant impact on your coffee business's supply chain; shifts in legislation and societal opinion relating to asylum seekers would significantly impact your charity.

For the scenario in the diagram, the two driving forces are from the political and social spheres:

Social openness to receiving the gospel: We are uncertain about whether there will be an increase or decrease in Western openness to receiving the gospel, but either way, this would have a significant impact.

The political stance on religious freedom: We are uncertain about whether there will be an increase or decrease in Western religious freedom, but either way, this would have a significant impact.

3. Plot the driving forces on a Scenario Framework. Use your two driving forces to create a quadrant.

The diagram on the previous page shows the two driving forces for the church's possible future context in the West. The vertical line represents low to high levels of social openness to the gospel. The horizontal line represents low to high levels of religious freedom.

4. Name and explore the four scenarios across the quadrant. Now that you have identified and plotted your driving forces, your diagram reveals four potential scenario outcomes; one in each quadrant. These then need to be named and explored. For our scenario, the four quadrants have been named as:

The Persecuted Church: There is social antagonism towards the gospel and state-imposed limitations on churches. This would be a dystopian future, where the church suffers under challenges from both state and society.

The Irrelevant Church: There is social antagonism towards the gospel and state liberty for churches. This would be a mixed bag, where the church is free to practise the faith, but sees little response from its work.

The Resilient Church: There is social revival towards Christianity and state-imposed limitations for churches. This would be another mixed bag, where under intense state restrictions, huge numbers are coming to faith.

The Favoured Church: There is social revival towards Christianity and state liberty for churches. This would be a utopian future, where the church is free to practise the faith and sees huge responses to the gospel.

With these scenarios named, you can unleash your creativity and describe what it feels and looks like to be part of the church in each of the four quadrants. For example, for the Persecuted Church you may describe the emergence of house churches alongside the increased use of technology to be able to practise key elements of faith.

5. Take appropriate action. Once the four possible futures are imagined, you must think through what, if anything, you should be doing now, based on those potential futures. For example, as a church leader in the West, the example given makes me think, *Am I seeking to make resilient disciples who could persevere in the Persecuted Church?*

THINKING BIBLICALLY

Three biblical themes are of significance here.

First, there is a real danger in seeking to predict the future. Jesus warns us that things can change very suddenly (Luke 12:20), and similarly James warns, 'You do not even know what will happen tomorrow' (James 4:14a). Indeed, seeking to know the future through divination and sorcery is specifically prohibited in the Scriptures (Deuteronomy 18:9–12 and Galatians 5:19–20).

Second, God knows the future and sometimes wants to share elements of it. For example, Joseph in the Old Testament (Genesis 41:25) and Agabus in the New Testament (Acts 11:28), both by God's Spirit predict future famines, which helped people prepare. This fact, alongside the general wisdom of thinking about eventualities (Luke 14:28), should encourage us to pray for insight during a scenario-planning exercise.

Third, without opening a debate on eschatology and the millennium, Jesus has made some sure-fire predictions about the future. Namely that we will always have trouble in this life (John 16:33), but that he will return again 'like a thief in the night' (1 Thessalonians 5:2).

HOW DO I APPLY IT?

Simply take the worked example above and apply the process to your own organisation or project. This is best done with a diverse team, to ensure you consider a breadth of possible scenarios. For example, a culturally astute intellectual may highlight unseen trends that, if they continue, could be significant driving forces for you, whereas a people-connected, creative person may give insightful vocabulary as to how the quadrants will look and feel.

QUESTIONS FOR REFLECTION

What has happened in your life that you never saw coming?

Would a personal or organisational scenario-planning exercise have picked up the eventuality?

GO FURTHER

Read *Scenario Planning: A Field Guide for the Future* by Woody Wade.[18]

Thoughtful Negotiation

THE ZONE OF POSSIBLE AGREEMENT

CHRIS

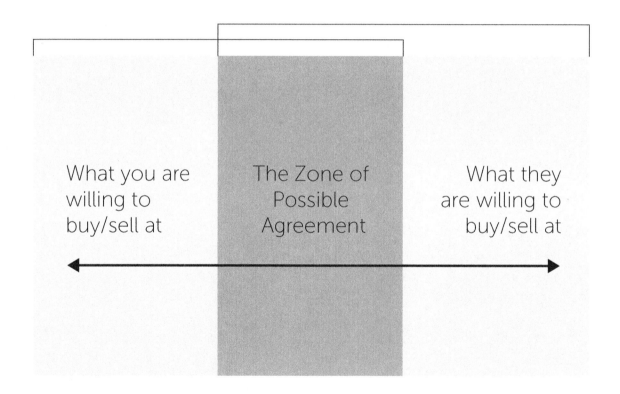

What you are willing to buy/sell at

The Zone of Possible Agreement

What they are willing to buy/sell at

SETTING THE SCENE

In the US, there is a consultancy that runs a very specific auction. They hold up a $20 bill and announce that the note will be auctioned in the same way as any other auction, with one exception: The highest bidder pays and wins, but the second highest bidder also has to pay. The auction will go up in $1 units, starting at $1.

The US consultancy that runs this auction says, 'It is very common to have final bids in the $30–$70 range, and our most successful auction sold a $20 bill for $407 (the final bids were $204 and $203). In total, we have earned over $10,000 running these auctions in business training over the last four years.'[19]

This modern-day parable helps point out the danger of what is known as 'non-rational escalation', which arises from poor negotiation skills. Good negotiation is essential for project leaders, who must navigate various agreements with all sorts of people.

WHAT'S THE BIG IDEA?

Whether we like it or not, buying and selling the right products or services, at the right time, for the right price, is often an essential ingredient to successful project leadership. Often integral to that ingredient is negotiating with others, to form agreements. Thankfully, the Zone of Possible Agreement (ZOPA) diagram is a helpful tool, summarising a negotiation planning process that will equip you to form better agreements.

This negotiation planning process can be broken down into four essential steps. These steps can be used before, during and after any negotiation meeting, as issues may become clearer throughout the working relationship. The example we will explore is a church attempting to rent out its spare land to a local business to use as car parking spaces.

1. WORK OUT EACH PARTY'S 'BEST ALTERNATIVE TO A NEGOTIATED AGREEMENT' (BATNA).[20]

A BATNA is essentially a plan B to attaining an agreement. Here, before making any agreements, work out not only what you may do if you don't reach an agreement, but also what the other party may do. For example, your plan B might be to approach other parties regarding renting your car parking spaces. You also know the party you're currently negotiating with does not seem to have a workable plan B, as there aren't any other car parking space options nearby. This information preps you with an understanding of the importance of any agreement to either party.

2. WORK OUT EACH PARTY'S SET OF INTERESTS AND AWARD EACH A PERCENTAGE OF IMPORTANCE.

In any negotiation, there will likely be one main interest, but also many other minor interests to be aware of. For example, with the car parking spaces:

Church interests

A. Gaining as much income as possible – 60 per cent

B. Any rental agreement not interfering with other activities at the church – 30 per cent

C. Forming a partnership with a local business – 10 per cent

The local business's interests

A. Securing parking spaces – 50 per cent

B. Having parking spaces for the next five years – 30 per cent

C. Paying as little as possible for the rental agreement – 10 per cent

D. Having safe and secure parking spaces – 10 per cent

While the scoring system is subjective and fails to incorporate the intricate links between the interests, it assists in a broad understanding of the weight of interests at play.

3. THINK ABOUT CREATING VALUE.

The idea here is about 'expanding the pie',[21] – in other words, with an awareness of both interests, bigger and better agreements can be proposed. For example, a five-year rental agreement for the car parking spaces could be discussed at a preferential rate, incorporating an agreement to invest in improving security at the car park, as well as the business agreeing not to use the car park on a set number of agreed dates.

4. WORK OUT THE 'ZONE OF POSSIBLE AGREEMENT' (ZOPA).[22]

Now you have an idea of the type of agreement that could be made and how important that agreement is to each party, you are ready to create the ZOPA diagram, or the assumed shared space between 'What you are willing to buy/sell at' and 'What they are willing to buy/sell at'. For example, you may know the cheapest you would accept the land being used for car parking spaces for five years, alongside the other agreements, would be $10,000, and estimate with further research that the highest the business would likely buy at would be $20,000. The ZOPA therefore would be between $10,000 and $20,000. Now you know the potential ZOPA, you're much better equipped to reach a beneficial agreement.

If selling something, working through these steps will help inform the first price you mention. This is significant, as it acts as an anchor for all future negotiation.

THINKING BIBLICALLY

There are three biblical principles to be aware of here. First, we should be aware of not approaching negotiations with a love of money, as that love is a root of all kinds of evil that can cause much grief (1 Timothy 6:10) and make us unfruitful in the Kingdom (Mark 4:19).

Second, it's okay to be shrewd. Although Jesus' advice to 'be as shrewd as snakes and as innocent as doves' (Matthew 10:16), is mission specific, it is also broad wisdom. That doesn't mean we should be stingy (Luke 16:8), but we should put our resources to work effectively (Matthew 25:14–30).

Third, it's not okay to play unfairly. If you're using tools like this to fleece the vulnerable for all you can get (Proverbs 14:31, Matthew 5:42), or in a contradictory approach to the fruit of the Spirit (Galatians 5:22–23), that's not okay. Much grace, wisdom and courage are needed if your employer expects you to behave like that.[23]

HOW DO I APPLY IT?

When applying the diagram, remember these two pointers:

You can always walk away. Be careful of entering agreements without the necessary thought. For example, it would likely be best to meet with several businesses regarding renting the church's car parking spaces before making any agreement.

The importance of the relationship. Negotiating is a relational art, so for big agreements, they're usually best done face-to-face. A temptation in negotiation is to force the agreement towards your end of the ZOPA. However, this is usually the wrong approach as it can damage your reputation and relationship with the other party. This, in turn, could result in future failings. For example, the business feels you have pushed them too hard on the rental fee, so they ignore the days they aren't meant to park there, don't agree to another five-year rental agreement at the end of the term and tell other local businesses how money focused you are.

QUESTIONS FOR REFLECTION

In the last negotiation you were in, how could the ZOPA process and diagram have helped you?

Do you tend to be too hard or too soft in negotiation? How could you improve that?

GO FURTHER

Read *Judgement in Managerial Decision Making*, 8th ed. and 'Nonrational escalation of commitment in negotiation', in *European Management Journal* by Max Bazerman and Don Moore.[24]

Taking Stock

THE SWOT ANALYSIS

CHRIS

S STRENGTHS

W WEAKNESSES

O OPPORTUNITIES

T THREATS

SETTING THE SCENE

In Greek mythology there's an unusual story about the skilled Daedalus and his inattentive son Icarus. Together they design and build an elaborate labyrinth to entrap a ghastly Minotaur, a creature with the body of a man and the head of a bull.

Afraid they will reveal the secrets of the labyrinth, Minos, the king of Crete, has Daedalus and Icarus imprisoned in a high tower. Daedalus, infamous for his intelligence, plots an escape. Observing the birds flying around the tower, he studies their mannerisms and patiently gathers all the feathers he finds. Joining them together with wax, he creates two pairs of wings, one for himself and the other for his son.

Before flying off to freedom, Daedalus forbids Icarus from flying too close to the sun as it will melt the wax. But Icarus, excited by the thrill of flying, starts rapidly elevating to salute the sun. Sure enough, the intense heat melts the wax on the wings, the feathers come loose, and Icarus plummets into the sea and drowns. A distraught and guilt-laden Daedalus names the place where he fell the Icarian Sea.

In 1990, Canadian economist Danny Miller coined the term the 'Icarus Paradox'.[25] Used in the sphere of organisational leadership, the term refers to the phenomenon of businesses suddenly failing after a period of success, when that failure is brought about by the same factors that initially brought their success. Miller drew on the idea of Icarus for this paradox because it was the same wings that helped Icarus to fly and escape his imprisonment that also led to his death.

WHAT'S THE BIG IDEA?

Things went wrong for Icarus when he denied the reality of the sun's heat and its impact on his wings. Defining reality is therefore a key skill if leaders are to lead well. Too often leaders believe false perceptions about how things are going. The SWOT diagram is a simple tool to help stimulate thought and expose any lies you're believing about how things are going. It uses two present- and internal-focused questions for your project or organisation:

S: What are the Strengths?
W: What are the Weaknesses?

and then two future- and external-focused questions for your project or organisation:

O: What are the Opportunities?
T: What are the Threats?

The idea is to use the diagram for any project or organisation you're helping to lead, personally or preferably as part of a team exercise. This is done by jotting down the answers in each quadrant to assess whether objectives are being and will be achieved.

THINKING BIBLICALLY

One way of seeing the opening chapters of the book of Revelation is Jesus' SWOT analysis of the seven churches. The church in Ephesus, for example, is strong at hard work, perseverance, testing claims and endurance, but weak at holding onto the love they first had for Jesus (Revelation 2:1–7). The church in Pergamum, on the other hand, is strong at being faithful, but weak at rejecting false teaching (Revelation 2:12–17).

Threats to the churches are raised too; the church in Smyrna is warned of future persecution (Revelation 2:10) and the church in Pergamum of future discipline (Revelation 2:16). And the church in Philadelphia, despite having little strength, has the opportunity of an 'open door' before them (Revelation 3:8).

Let this stir you to pray for God's eyes on the Strengths, Weaknesses, Opportunities and Threats that lay before you, and for the corresponding wisdom to respond, in whatever context you are leading.

HOW DO I APPLY IT?

Think about and jot down your organisation's or project's Strengths and Weaknesses. This will spark your ability to define reality for your organisation or project and share an honest assessment, such as:

'Our income is strong at the moment, but we can't let that blind us to our need to focus on improving customer care.'

'Despite the pain of losing several great staff members recently, 90 per cent of us are still here. With the great sense of trust we've built up over the years, we can work hard together to recruit the next right people.'

Then, consider the external context within which you are working and the Threats and Opportunities that may arise as a result. The Strengths you defined can easily be lost if they're not held up to scrutiny. For example, many Christian ministries were strong at providing teaching resources by tape and CD but failed to see the Threat of these technologies disappearing and the corresponding Opportunity of transitioning to an online service.

QUESTIONS FOR REFLECTION

What are the Strengths, Weaknesses, Opportunities and Threats of the organisation you help lead?

What is one urgent and important action for you to take away from this exercise?

GO FURTHER

Read *Are You Doing the SWOT Analysis Backwards?* by Laurence Minsky and David Aron, hbr.org/2021/02/are-you-doing-the-swot-analysis-backwards.

Facts Are Your Friend

MICHAEL PORTER'S FIVE FORCES
ANDY

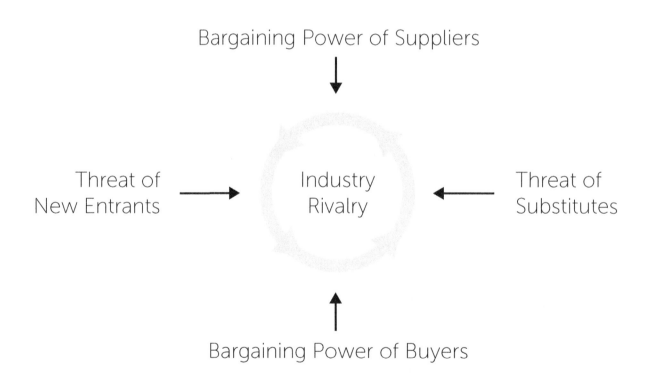

SETTING THE SCENE

I find entrepreneurs' stories fascinating.

Their ability to start something from nothing is an incredible feat. A few years back I read Phil Knight's book *Shoe Dog*, an autobiography of how he started the global brand Nike.[26]

It all started one day when he was out for a jog and had a crazy idea to set up a US company selling good-quality, but cheap, athletic shoes imported from Japan. The book charts his adventures as he travels to Japan to place his first order, and the story recounts the many challenges Knight encountered, including faulty trainers, legal challenges, equity issues, broken agreements and distribution problems.

Today, the 'swoosh' symbol is immediately recognisable as the globally successful brand Nike, but it's easy to miss the entrepreneurial story behind it.

Successful companies often have stories of twists and turns, ups and downs, with moments where their destiny hangs on a knife-edge. And even when big brands look like they are here forever, they can also be gone in a moment. Just think of Borders, PanAm, Blockbuster and Woolworths.

WHAT'S THE BIG IDEA?

Harvard Business School professor Michael E. Porter devised the Five Forces model to help analyse how competitive an environment is for any given company in any given industry.[27] No matter what the business, these five external forces determine the profitability of a company.

1. Industry Rivalry. This is the number of companies delivering a similar service or product. When there are more companies operating in a similar space, there is more competition and a stronger likelihood of another company undercutting your company's prices.

2. Threat of New Entrants. The long-term profitability of a company is also determined by how easy it is for new companies to enter the market as competitors. For example, if a competitor can quickly and cheaply enter the market, then your company is less stable.

3. Bargaining Power of Suppliers. Dependence on raw materials or qualified staff also impacts your company's long-term profitability. If there are multiple suppliers offering the resources you need, then you are more stable than if there are a limited number of suppliers who have the power to increase the cost you pay for their resource.

4. Bargaining Power of Buyers. If your company has a small client base buying expensive products or services, then your clients have more power to negotiate for lower prices. If, on the other hand, you have a large number of clients who purchase regularly for inexpensive products, then your company can more easily increase profitability.

5. Threat of Substitutes. Finally, if similar products or evolutions of products or services come to market, then your company will be more vulnerable to competition.

The Five Forces framework is a big-picture tool, designed to be used by companies. It is also not without its critics. One major issue is that it fails to consider government impact, such as legislation and tax rates. And there are some other concerns too. For example, some companies straddle several industries, and some industries aren't as heavily impacted by all five forces. However, Porter's Five Forces is helpful in enabling a company to understand and monitor the landscape, discovering how they are positioned competitively.

THINKING BIBLICALLY

When it comes to business models, it's hard to extrapolate lots of biblical examples, but the story of the twelve spies returning from Canaan illustrates the importance of doing the research. The spies describe how the land 'does flow with milk and honey' (Numbers 13:27) and that those who live there are strong and have fortified cities (Numbers 13:28). The spies have gleaned all the necessary data.

Caleb has staked out the land and is all set to move. He says, 'We should go up and take possession of the land, for we can certainly do it' (Numbers 13:30).

But the rest of the scouting crew don't want to take the land, even though God has promised it to them. They end up changing the data, giving Israel a bad report of the land. They go as far as to say that giants live in the land and the people of Israel are like grasshoppers in comparison!

Whatever we are doing in the business world, facts are our friend, and understanding the profitability of a business venture is wise.

HOW DO I APPLY IT?

If you are leading in business, then this tool helps you to look at the stability of the business and the profitability of new products and services. The tool helps you discern where the power lies and therefore where the strengths and weaknesses of the business lie.

To apply it, simply work through each of the five forces, using them as prompts to think through the strengths and weaknesses. This can be a particularly helpful activity when you are looking at expanding into a new area.

And although you may not be involved in a business as such, the framework could be used to think through the long-term profitability of a church-based coffee shop or a community project. It will help you discern the level of risk for any given project.

QUESTIONS FOR REFLECTION

What external factors might it be helpful for you to think through for the businesses or projects you are leading?

Where have you failed to consider external factors previously? How might considering such factors resulted in a different outcome?

GO FURTHER

Read *Competitive Strategy: Techniques for Analysing Industries and Competitors* by Michael E. Porter.

Who's In?

STAKEHOLDER ANALYSIS
ANDY

	LOW POWER	HIGH POWER
HIGH INTEREST	Subjects Involve	Players Collaborate
LOW INTEREST	Crowd Inform	Context Setters Consult

SETTING THE SCENE

A man was reaching a significant birthday, his fiftieth. The family agreed to throw him a surprise party, and so the planning began in earnest. The venue was booked. The food was ordered. The wine was selected. The decorations were purchased, and most importantly, the invites were sent out.

Two days before the big party, the family came together to run everything through and go over their checklists. It was at this point there was a significant realisation.

Nobody had actually invited the birthday boy!

(Thankfully he was free and able to come along!)

WHAT'S THE BIG IDEA?

When we're leading a project, sometimes we can forget to include the most important person involved. Stakeholders are the people who can impact a project, who have a 'stake' in the project's success. There are always internal stakeholders (who are part of the team) and external stakeholders (such as a local politician). Before a project starts, many organisations do an analysis to help them better understand who is involved, how involved they will be and how best to manage their involvement.

A common diagram used in this process is the Stakeholder Analysis Grid which maps Power over Interest. In this diagram, Power is defined as the influence a stakeholder has on the project. This Power normally revolves around decision-making, budgets and resources. Interest is about the level of concern, not just in the project itself, but in the project's results. This tool helps to map stakeholders into four groups.

THE PLAYERS
(HIGH POWER, HIGH INTEREST)
These are the most important stakeholders. They are the primary driving force behind the project. It is vital, if your project is to succeed, that this group are kept on-board. They are your priority group. Their expectations must be managed carefully, and they need to be kept informed so that they are fully engaged as the project develops.

THE CONTEXT SETTERS
(HIGH POWER, LOW INTEREST)
These stakeholders may have little interest in the project, but they need to be kept satisfied because they have both

the power to keep things moving and to derail things. Their expectations and needs must be understood and managed. This group need to be informed, but they will not appreciate overcommunication on every detail.

THE SUBJECTS
(LOW POWER, HIGH INTEREST)

This group may be interested in the project, but they do not have much power to move the project forward. Where possible, there should be an opportunity for them to share their input, even if it isn't implemented. This group can be helpful in promotion of the project. They need to be kept informed and may have some helpful observations.

THE CROWD
(LOW POWER, LOW INTEREST)

The final group are your lowest priority. They neither have much interest nor much capability to help. It is often difficult to identify the knowledge and input they could potentially offer. They only need periodic updates.

THINKING BIBLICALLY

Nehemiah says, 'Come, let us rebuild the wall of Jerusalem, and we will no longer be in disgrace' (Nehemiah 2:17b). The vision is set.

But as we know from the story, the process of rebuilding the walls is far from straightforward! There is complaining from his people and external threats.

Nehemiah understood the idea of stakeholders. When you read through his book, you can easily list these different people. For example, there is King Artaxerxes, who would have been a Context Setter. He has high power, providing the resources, but doesn't own the vision, which is Nehemiah's. Then there are the builders. Masterfully, Nehemiah assigns people to work on the wall nearest to where they live. The builders are the Players with high power and high interest.

This understanding of stakeholders is partially why Nehemiah is able to complete the rebuilding of the walls in just fifty-two days!

HOW DO I APPLY IT?

Whatever kind of project you are working on, whether it be a business launching a new product or a community fun day, there are three steps to carrying out a stakeholder analysis. Ideally these would take place before the project officially begins.

Step 1. List the stakeholders. The more comprehensive the list, the more you can be sure you haven't missed anyone, like the birthday boy in our story!

For a business launching a new project, the list may include the design team, executive staff, database managers, the marketing department and PR consultants. For a community fun day, the list may include volunteers, philanthropists, the civic office, the safeguarding officer and a graphic designer.

Step 2. Map the stakeholders on the diagram according to their power and interest. This gives you a clearer idea of who your Players are, as these are the key people for you to collaborate with.

Step 3. Create a spreadsheet with a clear plan for how you will manage each stakeholder. This should include detailing, where possible, their role, their motivations, their priorities in regard to the project and how best and how frequently to communicate with them.

QUESTIONS FOR REFLECTION

Who are the main stakeholders in your business/charity/church?

How aware are you of them, and do you communicate with them effectively?

What new habits could you form that would help your key stakeholders stay on board?

GO FURTHER

See more on this tool at tools4dev.org/resources/stakeholder-analysis-matrix-template.

Careful Change

MCKINSEY'S 7-S FRAMEWORK

CHRIS

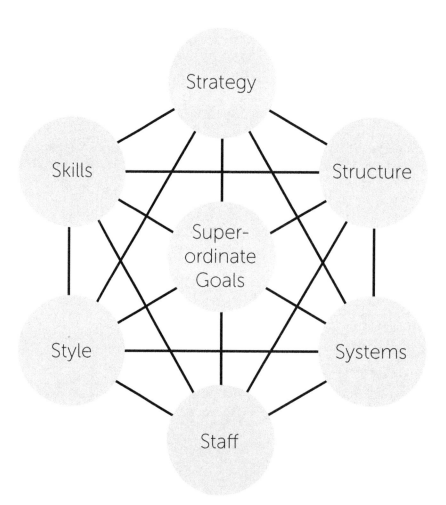

SETTING THE SCENE

One of the earliest versions of *The Parable of the Blind Men and an Elephant* is found in the Buddhist text *Tittha Sutta*, written around 500 BC. The story goes that a group of blind men, who have never come across an elephant before, imagine what the elephant is like by touching it.

Each blind man feels a different part of the elephant's body, such as an ear or the tusk, and describe the elephant based on their limited experience. The conflict in the story comes when each blind man can't conceive of why their experience of the elephant is so different from everyone else's.

Although the parable has inherent weaknesses,[28] it nevertheless remains a helpful picture for how, at times, we see things from a limited perspective. As leaders it is critical to step back and see the broader, holistic implications for our decisions. This is especially true when we are looking to enact change in our organisations.

WHAT'S THE BIG IDEA?

Once a needed organisational change has been identified, it's critical that all areas of your organisation are evaluated to understand how the identified change should be accomplished effectively.

First explained in the article 'Structure is not organisation',[29] McKinsey's 7-S framework provides three 'hard' organisation elements to consider when instigating change. These 'hard' elements are easy to identify and influence:

Strategy: This is your organisation's plan of how it will achieve its objectives. For example, an airline may seek to offer the cheapest fares.

Structure: This is how the people and roles in your organisation are arranged. For example, a small church may have an informal, non-hierarchical structure.

Systems: These are the core procedures that make your organisation operate. For example, the staff at a burger restaurant will carry out routine activities to run their drive-through, dine-in and delivery systems.

Then there are four 'soft' organisation elements, which are less identifiable and controllable:

Superordinate Goals: These were later termed 'Shared Values' and refer to the core values of the organisation, what it stands for, or what holds it together. For example, Disneyland seeks to create 'The happiest place on earth.'

Style: This is the way that things are done in an organisation. For example, a car dealership may have a highly pressurised sales culture.

Staff: This is the number and type of employees or volunteers in an organisation. For example, a school may have fifty full-time equivalent (FTE) employees.

Skills: These are the distinct and dominant capabilities of the organisation. For example, a tech company might be known for the outstanding quality and innovation of its products.

The idea is to work through each of these seven elements and the implications for them when seeking to implement change – asking of each S, how will this be impacted? For example, as a church leader I was keen to initiate hybrid (online and in-person) church gatherings as a result of the restrictions surrounding the COVID-19 pandemic. Failing to use the 7-S model at the diagnostic stage, I didn't realistically appreciate the implications this would have for the workload of our Staff, the need to improve related Skills, and the effect the cameras at our gatherings had on our Style. Applying the 7-S model beforehand would have ensured a smoother change process.

The framework is shown in a web, usefully demonstrating the interconnected nature of all the elements. If you picture the 7-S model as a wheel,[30] failure to consider just one or two of the elements will result in a somewhat bumpy strategic change.

THINKING BIBLICALLY

The Scriptures reveal a God whose plans are full of incredible holistic oversight. He created a fine-tuned world full of vegetation that would provide a continual globally sufficient supply, able to cater for today's earth of eight billion residents (Genesis 1:28–31).

In the Old Testament he gave his people the Law, which incorporated incredibly meticulous instructions for their and others' wellbeing, such as creating a culture where foreigners weren't mistreated (Exodus 22:21) and giving instructions for the prevention of the spread of mould (Leviticus 14:33–48).

Even when Jesus cleared the temple in righteous anger, 'he overturned the *tables* of the money changers', but only overturned 'the benches of those who sold doves' (Matthew 21:12, emphasis mine), likely so the birds weren't harmed in the process.

Indeed, Jesus' timing of coming to earth was such that it allowed the disciples and early church apostles relatively safe travel throughout the Roman world (Acts 23:23–25), ensuring the message of the gospel would spread at a rapid rate (Acts 19:10).

It is therefore godly to seek to be aware of the holistic implications of change, ensuring we consider others in the process (Philippians 2:3, Hebrews 10:24).

HOW DO I APPLY IT?

Much like a sculptor's chisel or a surgeon's knife, the usefulness of the 7-S model depends primarily on the skill of its handler. However, because it is memorable, it's an easy tool to bring into meetings where a potential future change is discussed, no matter how big or small.

When applying the model, it's important to remember that it's an internally focused model; it doesn't incorporate any considerations of change for the external environment. It could therefore also be helpful to think about external implications for change alongside this model. For example, organisations will talk of a triple bottom line, where the implications of change are considered not just in terms of internal profit but also externally: people (the wider community) and planet (the environment).

QUESTIONS FOR REFLECTION

Have you ever felt overlooked when a change was implemented? How did it make you feel?

What change are you currently considering or working on that you could apply the 7-S model to?

GO FURTHER

Read *Structure Is Not Organization* by Robert H. Waterman, Thomas J. Peters and Julien R. Phillips.

Spreading Speeds

THE INNOVATION ADOPTION CURVE

ANDY

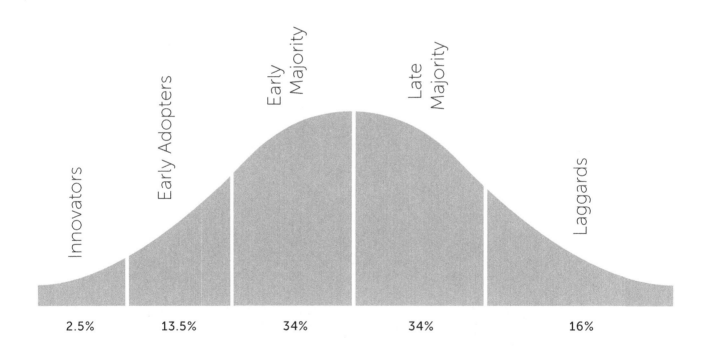

SETTING THE SCENE

One of the big issues for any parent today is when they should allow their child to have their own phone. My kids are desperate for their own phones. Before they were even in primary school, they were mimicking my wife's phone calls, using Lego bricks as pretend handsets.

I hit my teenage years in the 1990s. There were no mobile phones. Those that did exist were big and clunky and certainly not available to children. Instead, I grew up with one landline in the house and no other means of digital communication. The phone was a source of conflict because only one person could use it at a time, and until the invention of 'call waiting', a sibling could block the line for hours.

I remember when my friend first got a pager. A whole new world had opened up as his parents could now send us a limited number of words via text. He couldn't reply but had to find a phone box to call them back. As I hit university, mobile phones tipped. Everyone was getting one. They were still clunky and had no internet connection and no camera. I prided myself on being one of the last of my peers to get a mobile phone. I was a laggard.

The best thing about it? I can tell my kids that I didn't get a phone until I was twenty-one, and so they'll also have to wait!

WHAT'S THE BIG IDEA?

The Innovation Adoption Curve (which is also known as the Diffusion of Innovation Theory) breaks people down into groups based on their willingness to adopt new ideas. It was developed by professor of communication studies Everett M. Rogers who used the bell-curve diagram to show how quickly the market share will reach the saturation level as successive groups of consumers adopt a new technology.[31] It also helps us understand how ideas spread and the rate at which this happens.

The first stage of the curve shows the groups who adopt initially. The highest point indicates when the majority of people have adopted an idea, and the tail shows the continued adoption through a people group. The curve is often used in marketing to illustrate the potential growth of a product but can also be used to plot social uptake of an idea or attitude.

The curve has five categories.

INNOVATORS
An estimated 2.5 per cent of the population, the Innovators, are those that are willing to take risks and try new things. They will try things first, even when they may not have been fully tested. They are aware that not everything they adopt will reach mass-market appeal. They may be creators of new ideas and are often thought leaders in their field. They help to create a buzz around a new idea.

EARLY ADOPTERS

Early Adopters are still risk takers but more risk-averse than Innovators. Representing 13.5 per cent of the population, they tend to be more informed than Innovators and make reasoned decisions. They help push a new idea or product out further and tend to have cultural influence. They understand the need for change and help validate what the Innovators have pioneered.

EARLY MAJORITY

This third group comprises 34 per cent of the population. They are reasonably risk-averse and want to be sure they are adopting the right things. They are happy to wait until there is evidence but still adopt ideas sooner than the average person. They are often connected with Early Adopters and listen to their opinions.

LATE MAJORITY

This group are more sceptical and require more evidence than the first three groups before adopting new products, ideas or trends. Comprising 34 per cent of the population, they are more resistant to change, have less connection with Innovators and Early Adopters, and tend to adopt things because everyone else has.

LAGGARDS

The final group is the Laggards, making up 16 per cent of the population. They don't like risk, prefer traditional ideas and methods and dislike change. In regard to technology, this group can typically be the elderly. Often, by the time a product is being adopted by the Laggards, the product is entering decline.

It's important to note two things. First, that some people may be Early Adopters when it comes to a new piece of technology but a Laggard when it comes to adopting a new societal attitude. People do not necessarily sit in the same group for everything; it depends on what is being adopted. Second, sociologists make generalisations according to income, age and education around some of the characteristics of each category of people. These can be helpful, but they are only generalisations.

THINKING BIBLICALLY

'So when Peter went up to Jerusalem, the circumcised believers criticised him and said, "You went into the house of uncircumcised men and ate with them"' (Acts 11:2–3).

Peter did what no committed Jew at the time would have done. He entered the house of a Gentile and then broke bread with him.

This happened after he had received the vision from God of a sheet of 'unclean' food with the command to 'eat'. This moment changed the trajectory of the church, as Jesus' followers moved from being a Judaic movement to accepting all.

Peter was an innovator. And we see in Acts 11 that his actions were not received well by all. The idea that Gentiles could be part of God's family took time to be accepted by the entire Christian community.

HOW DO I APPLY IT?

As you lead projects, this diagram reminds us that not everybody will get on board with what you are doing straight away. If you are looking to do something new, you will often have to consider how the project will be accepted by those you are working with.

It's important to identify your audiences and make sure that you are communicating with them effectively.

- Who are the Innovators? How will you share the project with them? How will you harness their energy?
- Who are the Early Adopters? You will need them to buy in to the project if you are going to get momentum to carry it forward.
- Who are in the Early Majority and Late Majority groups? When and how will you communicate with them?
- Who are the Laggards? You may not be able to get them on board for a while. It's important to be aware of who they are and to anticipate their resistance to change.

When we are explaining the vision of the project, different audiences will need different communication. For example, the Early Majority will want as much information as possible so that they understand and appreciate how the project works.

In a business or church leadership team you may have people in all of the areas across the curve. Talking through this diagram and allowing people to self-identify where they are could be a good exercise to share both excitement and concern.

QUESTIONS FOR REFLECTION

Which category would you place yourself in when it comes to the project you are currently leading? Why?

What audiences are represented on your leadership team?

What are some of the pros and cons of each group?

GO FURTHER

Read *Diffusion of Innovations* by Everett M. Rogers.

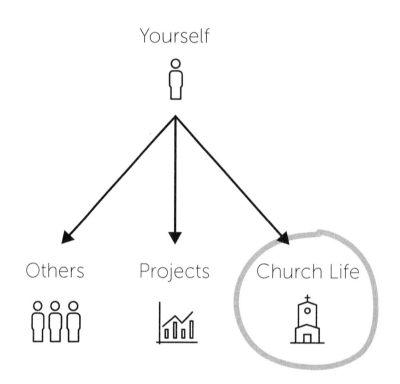

Section 4

LEADING CHURCH LIFE

It doesn't matter if you're leading a family or a business, if you're leading thousands or can barely lead yourself, every Christian is called to play a part in Jesus' leadership project: the local church. This section is to equip you in understanding how to effectively bring your leadership gifts to serve your local church family's mission.

LEADING CHURCH LIFE UPWARDLY:
Diagrams for Theological Understanding

LEADING CHURCH LIFE INTERNALLY:
Diagrams for Thriving Disciples

LEADING CHURCH LIFE EXTERNALLY:
Diagrams for Missional Impact

Reaching Righteousness

THE JUSTIFICATION/SANCTIFICATION GRAPH
CHRIS

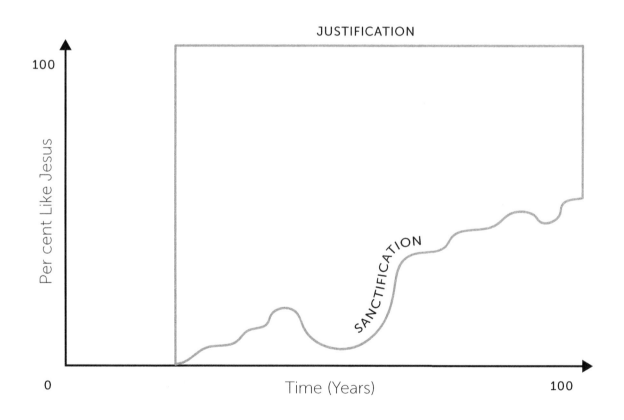

SETTING THE SCENE

In the summer of AD 386, Augustine came face to face with the depths of evil in his heart, resulting in a moment of deep spiritual agony. He was led to read Romans 13:13, which speaks about the sin he was tormented by, and he was converted to Christ in that moment. In his own words, 'All the gloom of doubt vanished away.'

In 1519, Martin Luther was haunted by the term 'righteousness of God' in Romans 1:17; 'For I hated that word "righteousness of God" ... I raged with a fierce and troubled conscience.' As Luther grappled with the text, he understood that the righteousness of God was a gift of God, given by faith, leaving him to feel he 'had entered paradise itself through open gates.'[1]

In 1740, Susanna Wesley, the mother of John and Charles, received communion with the exultation, 'The blood of our Lord Jesus Christ which was given for thee', and wrote, 'These words struck through my heart, and I knew that God for Christ's sake had forgiven me all my sins.'[2]

In 1850, Charles Spurgeon, aged fifteen, stumbled into a church and was picked out by the preacher. 'Young man,' the preacher said, 'you look very miserable, and you always will be miserable – miserable in life and miserable in death ... Young man, look to Jesus Christ. Look! Look! Look!' Spurgeon later wrote, 'And I did look ... and I could have risen that instant, and sung with the most enthusiastic of them, of the precious blood of Christ, and the simple faith which alone looks to him.'[3]

Separated by hundreds of miles and hundreds of years, all four of these characters were wracked by an awareness of their guilt before God. But through revelation, study, communion and preaching, each found they had been justified by faith, through Christ alone.

WHAT'S THE BIG IDEA?

One of the great travesties of our Christian lives is that we tend to approach God on the basis of our *sanctification* (our attempts to be holy) rather than our *justification* (being made right with God by the blood of Jesus). Therefore, when we think things are going well, we can quickly swell with pride. And when we think we're not following Jesus as we should be, we tend to avoid communing with him. The Bible shows us that Jesus made us right before God, and we can therefore consistently come to God with a humble confidence.

It is from the secure foundation of justification that we pursue sanctification, seeking to slowly become more like Jesus every day of our lives. The Justification/ Sanctification graph visually outlines this process.

The x-axis shows that at one point in our lives – just like Augustine, Luther, Susanna Wesley and Spurgeon – we are instantaneously justified; we are made righteous before God by faith in what Jesus has done for us. Whether we were consciously aware of that moment or not, it instantaneously makes us 100 per cent like Jesus, as displayed on the Justification line. This 'justified' status continues throughout all time, even beyond our physical death.

However, although we may have been made 100 per cent like Jesus, we know we don't live 100 per cent like Jesus. The Sanctification line on the diagram therefore represents our lifelong journey of becoming more and more like Jesus. Clearly this is just one roadmap, and everyone's journey will look different. This example of Sanctification includes lots of ups and downs, but also a gradual upwards move, which should reflect most believers' lives. The Sanctification line then shoots up at the point of death, when suddenly the Sanctification matches the Justification.

THINKING BIBLICALLY

There are five theological truths embodied within this diagram.

1. Justification is by faith alone. Many of us will be familiar with the phrase 'Just as if I'd never sinned', as a way to remember the meaning of 'justified'. However, it actually sells us short. According to the Bible, justification not only removes the stain of our sin (1 Corinthians 6:11), but it also gives us the righteousness of God (Philippians 3:9). The Bible is also clear that justification can only be received by faith (Romans 3:24, 5:21, Ephesians 2:8–9).

2. Sanctification is a process. 2 Corinthians 3:18 puts it like this: 'And we all, who with unveiled faces contemplate the Lord's glory, are being transformed into his image with ever-increasing glory, which comes from the Lord, who is the Spirit.' It's helpful to be aware that the Bible also describes us as already being sanctified (1 Corinthians 6:11) because God will continue the process until it is complete at our death (1 John 3:2).

3. True sanctification only begins when we first trust in Jesus. Anyone can make improvements in the way they live, but ultimately if these improvements don't originate in Jesus, they don't make us like him (Romans 3:22–24, Hebrews 11:6).

4. Sanctification usually increases through life. Because God is the ongoing committed initiator of our sanctification (Philippians 2:13), if we continue in obedience, we will grow more like Jesus as time passes (Philippians 3:12, 2 Corinthians 3:18). This doesn't necessarily mean we're conscious of an increased sanctification. Indeed, paradoxically, a lack of awareness of the work of sanctification in our life may itself be a sign of its increase, as was the case for Job (Job 42:1–6).

5. Sanctification is only completed upon our death or Jesus' return. 1 John 1:8 says, 'If we claim to be without sin, we deceive ourselves and the truth is not in us.' Therefore, we continue to confess our sins (Luke 11:4, 1 John 1:9), in our journey to be more like Jesus until we meet him, face to face, when we will be fully sanctified (1 John 3:2, Revelation 21:27).

HOW DO I APPLY IT?

There are two critical application points here:

1. Relate to God based upon your justification. Hebrews 4:16 says, 'Let us then approach God's throne of grace with confidence, so that we may receive mercy and find grace to help us in our time of need.'

Usually, our times of need are accompanied by a lack of confidence, and so we approach God in that spirit. However, the author of Hebrews calls us in those moments to approach God confidently. Like a child who has fallen and grazed their knee, we can run to God as a loving Father, confident he will provide compassion and practical care.

2. Work *with* Jesus for greater sanctification. When I was a young child, I would 'help' my mum water the garden. Pompously pouring out my tiny flowery watering can, I was proud of my efforts, completely ignorant to the hose pipe my mum was quietly uncoiling behind me.

Although we are commanded to play our part in becoming more like Jesus – by straining and striving forward (Luke 13:24, Hebrews 4:11) – it's critical to rest in the truth that Jesus is doing the real heavy lifting (Galatians 3:3, 1 Thessalonians 5:23). Our journey may be marked by sudden breakthroughs or serious setbacks, but we can be confident Jesus is always there to work with us, making us more like him.

Leading effectively in church life means creating a culture in which justification and sanctification are equally emphasised. This looks like Christian communities being imbibed with a strong conviction of their justification by faith, which itself produces an encouraged sanctification of obedience (Romans 1:5).

QUESTIONS FOR REFLECTION

How easy do you find it to relate to God as justified?

What does increasing sanctification look like in church life?

Does your church equally emphasise justification and sanctification? How might you redress the balance?

GO FURTHER

Read *Finally Alive* by John Piper.[4]

Crossing the Contextual River

THE INTERPRETIVE JOURNEY

ANDY

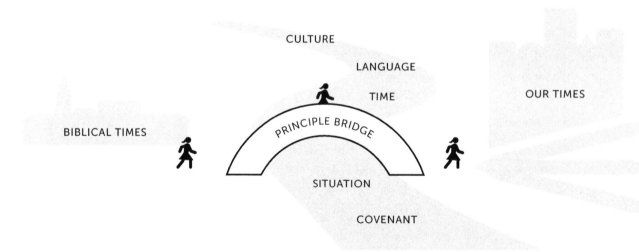

SETTING THE SCENE

I was gripped when I first started reading Dean Karnazes' book *Ultramarathon Man*.[5] He begins by describing a random conversation with a pizza delivery man. It's nearing midnight, and Dean is ordering pizza for himself. However, instead of ordering a pizza for one, he orders a family-sized pizza. Then he goes on to order not just one piece of cheesecake but an entire cheesecake. And on top of that he asks for a flask of coffee.

The already confused pizzeria man now asks for the delivery address, and Dean says he wants it to be delivered to the edge of a highway, miles from the nearest houses. The scene, as it unfolds, leaves the reader confused, too, until you discover that Dean is an ultramarathon runner, running 170 miles straight through day and night. He is desperate for calories to keep himself going. As the pizza is delivered, he rolls it up in one hand like a taco and carries on running off into the darkness, munching away.

Context is important!

WHAT'S THE BIG IDEA?

In their book *Grasping God's Word*,[6] Professor J. Scott Duvall and New Testament expert J. Daniel Hays use a simple diagram called the Interpretive Journey to help visually explain how we grapple with biblical text. Using four stages, the diagram helps us understand what the biblical text meant in its original context and what it means for us today.

BIBLICAL TIMES

To grasp this first step, we need to be aware of the preconceived ideas about the text we already have and question whether these are our own interpretations or based on the context in which the passage was written. We then need to answer the who, what, when, where, why and how questions, as we look to understand what the text meant for the original author and audience. Additionally, we need to be aware of two things. First, the genre of the text – this could be poetry, historical literature or prophetic prose. Second, we need to recognise where the text fits in the grand narrative of Scripture, such as when the Israelites settle in the Promised Land or during the persecution of the early church. So, for instance, if we bring genre and context together, the Old Testament book of Zechariah is prophetic literature, written to the Jewish people who were exiled in Babylon. This type of literature uses particular imagery and symbols that relate to the context of what was happening in the history of God's people at the time.

THE WIDTH OF THE RIVER

The river represents all that separates us from the original writers and audience. This includes language, the passage of time, geography and culture. For us, the river will be wider when we are looking at texts from further back in history, such as Genesis. Biblical passages in the New Testament would be represented by a narrower river as it's the new covenant and the time between their context and ours is less. Comparatively speaking, the early church would have read the Old Testament passages with a smaller conceptual river to cross, reading and interpreting these texts as part of a familiar narrative. Many of us, by contrast, read the Bible on our smart phones, in a very different setting to the Jewish or Greek contexts of the first century. Therefore, how we understand and interpret culture, language, time, situation and the meaning of covenant will be very different to the readers and listeners of the early church.

CROSSING THE PRINCIPLE BRIDGE

This involves us looking at principles in the passage that are timeless. These are principles found in the text that are not tied to the original culture or a specific situation and which are still relevant to the contemporary reader. Importantly, these principles will correspond with the rest of Scripture. It's helpful to think through what the text shows us about God's character, the human condition and God's rescue plan.

OUR TIMES

Once over the bridge, we need to apply the principles to our lives. How do they challenge the way we live today? This is more than an intellectual exercise. With the help of the Holy Spirit, we ask, 'Now what?'

THINKING BIBLICALLY

At age twelve, King Josiah began to tear down the altars of other gods and smashed up their carved images and idols. And at twenty-six, he raised some money, recruited a team of carpenters, stone masons and artists, and started repairing the temple.

While the temple was being refurbished, the book of the Law was found, which commentators think could have been the book of Deuteronomy.[7] Josiah had the book read to him, and as it was read he began to weep and tear his royal robes.

Josiah discovered the covenant that the people of Israel had made with God. God had promised to be faithful to the Israelites, but the people had also promised to be faithful to him. And they had failed.

King Josiah firstly went to the prophetess Huldah to help him understand what God was saying. He then brought everyone together from across the land to hear him read the book aloud. The people gathered, and once he finished reading, the king committed to God that he'd live according to the promises his ancestors had made. And all the people who gathered did the same. Josiah had made the Interpretive Journey.

HOW DO I APPLY IT?

Whether you are leading a small group or running a youth ministry, the Interpretive Journey is a useful diagram to help those you are leading to explore the Bible. It aids them in seeing the journey they have to undertake to understand how the Bible is relevant for them today, particularly with some of the trickier biblical passages.

You might like to share the diagram on a PowerPoint or whiteboard when you are teaching or preaching, to help people understand the background information of the passage. It might also help people consider how they can apply it in their own devotional times.

QUESTIONS FOR REFLECTION

Which of the four steps in the Interpretive Journey are you strongest at? Weakest?

How could you develop your weakest step?

What level of confidence do those you lead have in applying the Interpretive Journey?

How can you best resource them and make it a consistent tool in church life?

GO FURTHER

Read *Grasping God's Word* by J. Scott Duvall and J. Daniel Hays.

Story Time

GOD'S BIG PICTURE
ANDY

1. THE STORY BEGINS

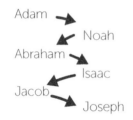

2. EGYPT TO THE PROMISED LAND

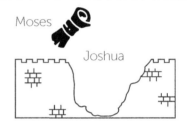

3. ISRAEL

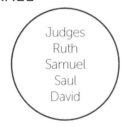

4. ISRAEL DIVIDED

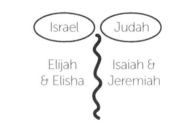

5. CAPTIVITY & RETURN

6. JESUS

7. CHURCH

8. REVELATION

HOPE

SETTING THE SCENE

Stories are everywhere. We often think of stories as being entombed in books and films, but the truth is, stories are all around us. The poet Muriel Rukeyser famously unpacked the idea that the universe is not really made of atoms but of stories.[8] Every day we receive dozens of stories just from the adverts that adorn street hoardings, our TV screens and our social media channels. It's fascinating how frequently advertisers don't even feature the product in the commercial; instead, they tell us a story rich in emotion that somehow connects with our very being.

Our news media also pumps us with stories whenever we glance at a screen or wade through a paper. Whichever incident is being reported, the coverage we choose to follow dictates the story that is being told. The reporters tell us who are the 'good guys' and who are the 'bad guys'. These stories saturate our lives.

And our history is a key aspect of the narratives we remember and adopt in our own lives, shaping how we see the world. Most days, we pass by the monuments and graveyards that punctuate our cities, towns and villages without a second thought. But these also tell a story, often influencing our national or family identity. These monuments remind us of our past, the cost of freedom, the heroes of history. And graveyards remind us of our future, our mortality. Commemorative monuments are nearly always built by the victors, reinforcing their perspective of the story. While stories feel integral to our very understanding of ourselves and the world, it is important to remember the many perspectives and interpretations there can be of any particular narrative.

WHAT'S THE BIG IDEA?

The Bible is a big book. Well, actually it's sixty-six books written in different languages, in different styles, by different people, in different countries, in different centuries. God has not simply given us a list of rules and regulations to follow, but a story for us to be a part of.

As I began reading the Bible with my kids, they would often have a perplexed look on their faces. They were discovering familiar stories about Moses, Esther, Daniel and Jesus, but they had no idea how they all fitted together. 'Did Jesus' dad have a really colourful cloak?' they asked. 'No,' I replied. 'That's a different Joseph.'

I drew this simple diagram to help them understand how the story of the Bible fits together, and I have found that many adults find it helpful too!

There are eight scenes:

1. The Story Begins. The book of Genesis sets out the story of the first few generations, from Adam and Eve to Joseph (the one with the cloak), concluding with Joseph settling with his brothers in Egypt.

2. Egypt to the Promised Land. Taking in the rest of the Pentateuch, this scene starts with the call of Moses, moves through to the giving of the Law, the walls of Jericho tumbling down and the arrival of the Israelites in the Promised Land.

3. Israel. From the times of the Judges all the way up to King Solomon, this third scene is the story of the first king, Saul, and the blossoming of Israel up until the reign of Solomon.

4. Israel Divided. From around 930 BC, this is the story of the Kingdom splitting, with Israel in the north and Judah in the south, and the corresponding prophets who spoke God's word to the people in that time. (The story begins in 1 Kings 12 and 2 Chronicles 10.)

5. Captivity and Return. This scene tells the story of the fall of Israel to Assyria and the fall of Judah to the Babylonian empire. It covers the lives of people such as Daniel (in Babylon) and Esther (in Persia) in foreign lands and the return of Nehemiah and others to their homeland.

6. Jesus. Following a long period of silence and the emergence of the Roman empire, Jesus comes on the scene. His story is told through Matthew, Mark, Luke and John.

7. Church. This is the place in the story where we find ourselves today. The book of Acts tells the story of the coming of the Holy Spirit, and the letters help us explore what following Jesus looks like.

8. Revelation. Finally, there is the bookend scene of a new heaven and a new earth. The story that began in a garden finishes in a city.

THINKING BIBLICALLY

In Matthew 4, Jesus is in the desert, fasting. We can imagine the hunger pains: that simplest of desires for food. And in the middle of Jesus' great time of need, Satan appears … the battle commences.

One of the things Satan does is to take Jesus to the highest point of the temple. He challenges Jesus, saying, 'If you are God's son, jump off' (paraphrased from verse 6).

Now what is incredible here is that Satan quotes Scripture at Jesus. He quotes God's promise that God will rescue him … that his angels will catch him.

I imagine Jesus standing right up to Satan as he speaks back, '"Scripture also says, 'Don't test God'"' (verse 7).

I find this exchange fascinating. Satan pulls God's words out of context and distorts the meaning to set his trap. It shows us just how important it is to understand the text as part of the grand narrative. By the Holy Spirit, Scripture shows us who we are and who we are called to be. Understanding the bigger story of Scripture helps us better understand the context of the verses we are reading.

HOW DO I APPLY IT?

When you are preaching, teaching or leading a Bible study, this diagram can be helpful to show people where the passage is located in the grand narrative. It's the kind of framework you could use on a PowerPoint before you preach, or you could print it out for people to insert inside their Bibles.

QUESTIONS FOR REFLECTION

How confident are those you lead in explaining the narrative of Scripture?

What has helped you better understand the context and flow of the Bible, and how could your journey practically help those you lead?

GO FURTHER

Check out *The Bible Course* via biblesociety.org.uk and *The Bible Project* via bibleproject.com.

Setting Expectations

KINGDOM ALREADY BUT NOT YET
CHRIS

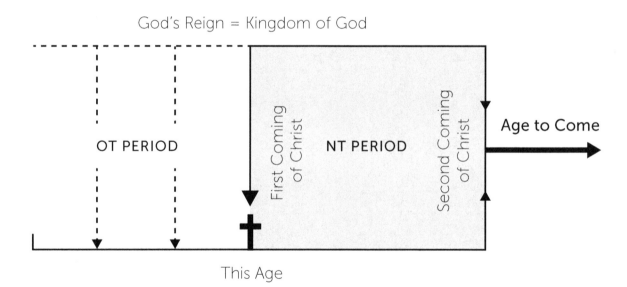

SETTING THE SCENE

The situation was getting desperate; due to a completely dysfunctional school that was later closed down, my parents were faced with an urgent need to find their eight-year-old, my big brother, a new school. But no matter how hard they tried, every door was closing. At the end of our rope again, Dad gathered us as a family around the table to ask for God's help. God's answer to this simple prayer time would be far more miraculous than we could ever have dreamed.

The very next day my dad found himself shouting out, 'Aberdour! Aberdour! Aberdour!' as he awoke bolt upright in the middle of the night. Perplexed by a word he had never heard before, he wrote the name on a bit of paper by the side of his bed, went back to sleep and forgot all about it.

Some days later, finding this obscure note, he remembered the incident and out of intrigue contacted directory enquiries (this was before our friend Google had all the answers). 'Do you have a listing for Ab – er – do - ur at all?' The bemused response: 'Just the one, sir. There is a junior private school in Burgh Heath with that name.'

Encouraged by the bizarre coincidence – Burgh Heath was not far from us – my father arranged a visit.

'I love it!' my dad beamed excitedly, in the headmaster's elaborate office. The school would so clearly be a perfect haven for his little boy. 'But …' he added cautiously, aware it was a private school, '… may I enquire about fees?'

The intimidating headmaster reached for a pen and discretely scribbled down an annual figure on a pad. (You know it's going to be bad news when someone feels the need to write that kind of information down.) My dad's face went a little pale as he glared at the sum that screamed, 'Not you buddy!' He made pleasantries and set off to his car.

But God was in this. Just as Dad was about to drive off, dismissing the incident as a bizarre coincidence and a waste of time, the headmaster came running out of his office and blocked the gateway. Still panting, he enquired, 'What was it you said you did again?' 'I'm a Methodist minister,' was the confused response. 'Come with me,' the headmaster said as he motioned with his finger.

The headmaster had suddenly been reminded of an unused bursary for ministers' sons, set up by the school's founder decades ago. As a result, both my brother and I went on to enjoy completely free schooling at Aberdour until we were thirteen!

Stories like this shouldn't shock us, but they do because we forget that the Kingdom of God comes when we pray for it.

WHAT'S THE BIG IDEA?

The paradox of the following two sentences summarises a tension all followers of Jesus should feel:

God wants us to expect and pray for his Kingly rule and reign to enter our here and now.

God wants us to patiently endure hardship until he returns with his Kingdom.

Theologian George Eldon Ladd uses the language of 'the Kingdom of God is already and not yet'.[9] His diagram helpfully depicts this tension, by outlining three periods or ages.

The first is the Old Testament Period, where the Kingdom of God is shown to be breaking into human history intermittently and imperfectly through broken lines.

The second is the New Testament Period, where the Kingdom of God is shown to have been inaugurated into human history by Jesus through a solid line and the cross.

The third is the Age to Come, where there is no distinction between the Kingdom of God and human experience, as the Kingdom of God has been consummated by the Second Coming of Christ.

The diagram therefore provides a helpful picture to help us believe for God's Kingdom now, but also to anticipate its final coming.

THINKING BIBLICALLY

When a pregnant mother feels a move of her unborn baby within her, or when a hungry boy smells the sweet aroma of his dinner being prepared, it triggers hope for something better to come.

The Bible teaches us to expect God's Kingdom but also to live in the reality of his Kingdom being 'already and not yet'.

It tells us that Jesus brought his Kingdom with him in a new way when he came to earth (Matthew 4:17), and that we should pray for more of it to come (Matthew 6:10). But it also teaches that our experience of the Kingdom will not be fully realised until this age comes to an end (Matthew 8:11, Revelation 21:4).

Therefore, in terms of our health we can expect Jesus to heal now (Matthew 10:1, 7–8, Acts 5:15–16), but we won't see everyone healed yet, as experienced by Jesus (Matthew 13:58) and the early church (1 Timothy 5:23, 2 Timothy 4:20). It follows that dying well is a part of the victorious Christian life (Ecclesiastes 3:2–3).

In terms of our finances, we can expect Jesus to provide for our needs now (Matthew 6:31–33, Philippians 4:19, 1 Timothy 6:8), but not make us materially wealthy (Matthew 6:19–20, Romans 8:17). Indeed, the New Testament teaches us that a desire for wealth is dangerous (1 Timothy 6:9–10).

In terms of our emotional experience, we can expect Jesus to give us joy now (Luke 2:10, Romans 14:17, Galatians 5:22), but not always make us happy (Acts 14:22, Philippians 3:10).

HOW DO I APPLY IT?

Shadrach, Meshach and Abednego are in a tight spot in Daniel chapter 3. They are about to be thrown into a blazing furnace for refusing to worship Nebuchadnezzar's gold statue. Their faith-filled response is outstanding: 'If we are thrown into the blazing furnace, the God we serve is able to deliver us from it, and he will deliver us from Your Majesty's hand' (Daniel 3:17).

They have utter confidence in God's ability to rescue them. God is not only 'able', but he 'will' rescue them. When we encounter difficulties, are we similarly full of confidence in God's ability to act?

However, Shadrach, Meshach and Abednego's statement doesn't end there. They continue, 'But even if he does not, we want you to know, Your Majesty, that we will not serve your gods or worship the image of gold you have set up' (Daniel 3:18). They also have confidence in God's sovereign care for them, and so regardless of what happens, they refuse to relinquish their resting trust in God and corresponding obedience. In the same way, when difficulties are encountered in church life, it's important to be full of confidence in God's sovereign care as we await Jesus' return, whatever happens.

QUESTIONS FOR REFLECTION

Do you encourage those you lead to expect God's Kingdom to break in?

Do you have a tendency to approach challenges in church life with a leaning towards the Kingdom Already or the Kingdom Not Yet? Why?

As a church community, what has been your greatest experience of the Kingdom Already?

GO FURTHER

Watch *The Bible Project*'s explanation of the Kingdom: bibleproject.com/explore/video/gospel-kingdom.

Preaching Dynamics

THE HOMILETIC KITE

CHRIS

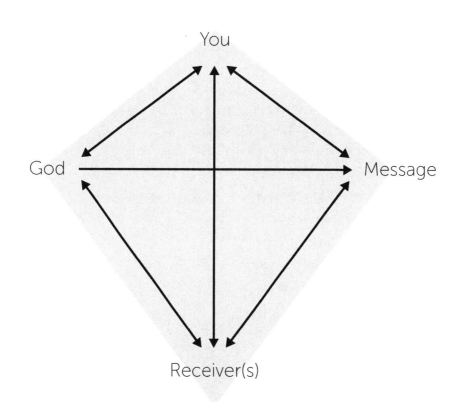

SETTING THE SCENE

The date is 9 April 1945; the location is Flossenbürg concentration camp in Germany. It's just one month before the surrender of the Nazis in World War II – an unusual setting for a pastor and theologian's last sermon. Dietrich Bonhoeffer is stripped naked and brought before the gallows, where he is to be hung for his involvement in an assassination attempt on Adolf Hitler. A captured RAF pilot hears Bonhoeffer proclaim his hope in Jesus: 'This is for me the end, the beginning of life.'[10]

Bonhoeffer had served as a pastor in London and then led an underground seminary in Finkenwalde, where he trained pastors who insisted that Christ, not the Führer, was the head of the church. After the seminary was closed down by the Gestapo, Bonhoeffer eventually became a double-double agent. He not only worked for the German military intelligence, but he was also serving the German resistance movement and in turn feeding information to the Western Allies, in hope of garnering their support. Throughout, he continued to try to express his faith in a challenging context. He remained an ardent believer in the power of preaching but recognised the importance of the Spirit's role in all that he taught: 'I will never be able to convert through the power of my sermon unless the Spirit comes and makes my word into the Spirit's word.'[11]

WHAT'S THE BIG IDEA?

The art of preaching, or homiletics, is much more than someone saying a few words about something in the Bible. There are four key elements involved.

YOU

Some believers have a specific gift to preach and teach (1 Peter 4:10–11, Romans 12:7, James 3:1, 1 Timothy 1:3), but all followers of Jesus help deliver God's message to others (Colossians 3:16, 1 Corinthians 14:26, John 20:21, Acts 8:4–5).

THE MESSAGE

This is the content of the message you are delivering, shaped around the gospel of Jesus Christ in the Scriptures (1 Corinthians 9:16). It could be a sixty-minute exposition of a verse from Romans or simply sharing the story of how you came to faith.

GOD

Preaching stands or falls on its accompaniment with God's power; without it, it's just like any other speech.

RECEIVER(S)

This could be a vast stadium crammed with people without faith or a handful of people at your local church.

The above four subjects are all intricately involved with one another, as outlined in the Homiletic Kite. Through the arrows, the diagram depicts the importance of the reciprocal relationship that you have with God, your message and the receivers of it, before, during and after your preaching.

THINKING BIBLICALLY

Most importantly, the diagram demonstrates God's commitment to be with you as you speak for him (Luke 12:11–12), as he inhabits his message (Isaiah 55:11) and works on the hearts of the receivers of his message (John 16:8). Indeed, the Homiletic Kite flies most effectively when you learn to use the powerful wind of God's mysterious Spirit (John 3:8, Acts 2:2).

It also displays the receiver's mutual relationship with you, the preacher (1 Corinthians 2:4–6), and the message (1 Thessalonians 1:5). The hoped-for consequences of the message being passed onto others (2 Timothy 2:2) and lived out (John 13:17) are displayed in the kite's ribbons.

HOW DO I APPLY IT?

The diagram is best applied by thinking through the four elements and how they interact with one another.

YOU

Before preaching, you might hear someone pray something like this: 'Lord, I ask you that the congregation wouldn't see Chris today, but just you.' Although I appreciate the sentiment of that prayer, it's nonsense. The hope, of course, is that as a result of the message, people will savour Jesus like a fine wine, but without the bottle to pour that wine, there's just a mess on the table. Professor of Preaching Haddon Robinson puts it like this, 'In the final analysis, listeners do not hear a sermon. They hear you.'[12]

For those who feel less confident about preaching, it can be tempting to come up with plenty of reasons why God can't use you to deliver his message. But the Bible is filled with stories of messed-up people who were funnels for God's message. Moses had a stuttering problem, Jeremiah and Timothy were too young, Elijah was suicidal, Jonah ran from God, Peter denied Christ, the disciples fell asleep while praying, and the Samaritan woman had multiple husbands.

It's essential to have a healthy awareness of your need for God's grace when passing on his word. Charles Spurgeon, arguably the greatest preacher of the modern era, said, 'I have still a sense of my own weakness, nothingness, and utter inability to do anything in and of myself – I pray God that I may never lose it.'[13]

THE MESSAGE

When you have an opportunity to share a message, its main content must be about Jesus. Otherwise, your message will be like a gift bag without a gift in it! The message must also move you; you're not delivering a lecture but a piece of spiritual dynamite that first must have detonated in your heart.

RECEIVER(S)

The receiver(s) of your message are in a macro and micro cultural moment, so bear this in mind as the message is prepared. Haddon Robinson put it well when he said, 'Imagine if Paul's letters to the Corinthians had been sent to the Philippians by mistake … Preachers … must be as familiar with the needs of their churches as they are with the content of their Bibles.'[14]

For the ribbons to flow out of the receiver(s), you need to be clear on what life changes you are encouraging your receiver(s) to seek.

GOD

It was said of Scottish minister Robert Murray McCheyne that when he appeared in the pulpit, even before he had uttered a single word, people would begin to weep silently. It's easy to forget how intricately involved God wants to be in your preaching process.

QUESTIONS FOR REFLECTION

How would you define the purpose of preaching?

What preaching has impacted you the most and why?

How could a greater awareness of God and the receivers of your message influence what you say?

What could you do to increase your awareness of God when you share his message?

GO FURTHER

Read *Evangelism in a Skeptical World: How to Make the Unbelievable News about Jesus More Believable* by Sam Chan.[15]

Read *Explosive Preaching: Letters on Detonating the Gospel in the 21st Century* by Ronald Boyd-MacMillan.[16]

Read *Preaching: Communicating Faith in a Sceptical Age* by Timothy Keller.[17]

Discipleship Space

HALL'S FOUR RELATIONAL SPACES
ANDY

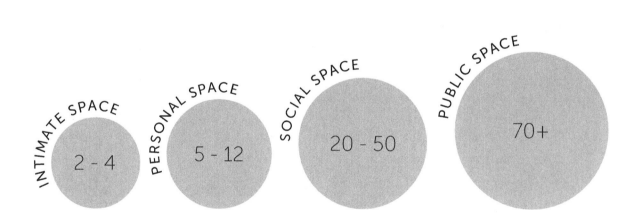

INTIMATE SPACE
2 - 4

PERSONAL SPACE
5 - 12

SOCIAL SPACE
20 - 50

PUBLIC SPACE
70+

SETTING THE SCENE

As a family we spent a year living in France. It was fascinating to live in a different culture. Although the UK and France are both Western and have much shared European history, they have very different ways of doing things. Navigating a different way of life is challenging, and it is even trickier when you're far from fluent in the language.

It was interesting to observe how the French build community. For example, they take a two-hour lunch break because community is built over food. The French subsidise sporting activities because they believe community is built through sport. And when you invite someone over, most likely the whole family will turn up because community is often built in family units.

WHAT'S THE BIG IDEA?

When we think about church, we often think primarily of our main gathering, normally on a Sunday morning with worship and a sermon. But most churches will have a variety of connection spaces during the week. They may be in-person or they may be online. They may include house groups, prayer meetings, luncheon clubs, social events and parent and toddler groups.

Anthropologist Edward T. Hall found that there are four relational spaces in which we build community.[18] As church leaders, if we want to be intentional in our discipleship, then understanding and using these four spaces is important.

PUBLIC SPACE: 70+ PEOPLE
Although there is often little interaction in this space, it can still be meaningful. A church service is a prime example of Public Space.

SOCIAL SPACE: 20–50 PEOPLE
Many churches lack this space. It's a space small enough for people to experience genuine community, but, at the same time, large enough to mobilise people for mission. Some churches and organisations call this space 'missional community' and are seeking to prioritise its place within church life.[19] It's in this social space that we make connections and discern who we might want to grow a deeper friendship with. It's also a safe space to invite those who are not yet part of a church community.

PERSONAL SPACE: 5–12 PEOPLE
This is where we experience close friendships. These people know a lot about us, although it's not usually a space in

which we will voice all of our innermost feelings. For many churches, this is often what we experience in a small group.

INTIMATE SPACE: 2–4 PEOPLE

This is where we share our deepest selves: our closest friendship, our marriage, or a prayer partnership or triplet.

When we think about discipleship, most churches think primarily about one or two spaces. We tend to think about the church service (the Public Space) and small groups (the Personal Space). We subconsciously believe that this is where the good stuff happens and that these two spaces will help people truly belong. However, commitment and participation happen in all four spaces. Joseph Myers, who applied Hall's thinking to the local church, argues that if you want to build a strong church community then you need to allow people to grow significant relationships in all four spaces.[20]

In leading ministries and churches, we often want to develop deep and meaningful conversations, but small talk and fun are also important for relationships to flourish. Genuine friendships can't be manufactured, but we can create the different spaces that enable social interaction.

THINKING BIBLICALLY

In the Gospels, people connected with Jesus in different spaces. It could be argued that Jesus strategically used different spaces to disciple people effectively.

Jesus used the Public Space when the crowds gathered to hear him speak. Large groups came to hear the Sermon on the Mount (Matthew 5–7) as well as when he miraculously fed the crowds of five thousand and four thousand on the hillside. After his ascension, the 120 believers praying with Peter (Acts 1:15) would also constitute a Public Space.

There seems to be a Social Space that Jesus creates with around seventy followers. In Luke 10, he sends out the seventy-two, but there is a sense that they have also been gathered together beforehand. It seems Jesus brings them together with a purpose for mission.

The Personal Space is the space Jesus created with the twelve disciples. He invested the majority of his time with this group, who had left their homes and families to follow him.

Finally, Jesus engaged with the Intimate Space with his inner circle of Peter, James and John. All three of their names appear together in the Gospels five times: when Peter's mother-in-law is healed (Mark 1:29–31); when Jairus's daughter is raised from the dead (Mark 5:37); at the transfiguration (Mark 9:2); at the Mount of Olives (Mark 13:3); and in the Garden of Gethsemane (Matthew 26:37).

HOW DO I APPLY IT?

Think through the spaces you create across your church or ministry during a week. Some will be structured spaces (like a house group), and some will be unstructured (like conversation over coffee after a service). What spaces are missing?

Plot these activities and opportunities for connection (both structured and spontaneous) across the different spaces on the diagram. What spaces are lacking, and how could you create connection points in those spaces?

If you help lead a small church, where a Public Space isn't possible, you might need to consider how your church activities could look different. For example, if your Sunday service usually has thirty-five people attending, why not have a more relaxed style of meeting, as it is serving a Social Space, rather than the Public Space? You might also want to find opportunities for your church to experience the Public Space, perhaps by joining with cross-church activities, such as Christian conferences, city-wide prayer or inter-church ministries.

Consider what you communicate about the spaces in your church. How might you explain to newcomers what church life looks like in the different spaces and how they can get involved? Can you identify individuals who are skilled at welcoming people in the different spaces? Why not talk to them about how they could encourage more people to connect with each other in that space.

QUESTIONS FOR REFLECTION

Which spaces do most of your church activities fit within? Why might this be?

Do you know of any other churches which function well in the spaces you struggle with? What might you be able to learn from them?

GO FURTHER

Read *The Search to Belong* by Joseph R. Myers and *Discipleship That Fits* by Alex Absalom and Bobby Harrington.[21]

Sensing the Seasons

THE LIFE CYCLE AND STAGES OF
CONGREGATIONAL DEVELOPMENT

CHRIS

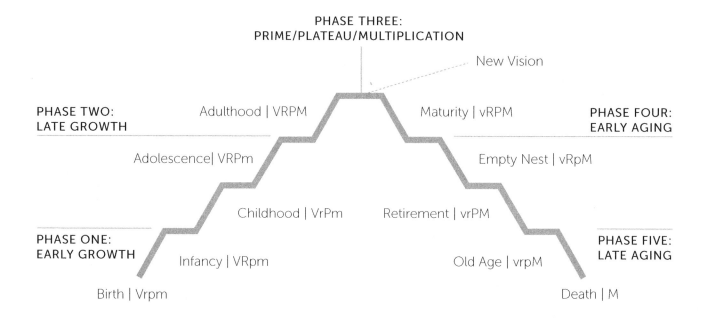

PHASE THREE:
PRIME/PLATEAU/MULTIPLICATION

New Vision

PHASE TWO:
LATE GROWTH

Adulthood | VRPM

Maturity | vRPM

PHASE FOUR:
EARLY AGING

Adolescence| VRPm

Empty Nest | vRpM

Childhood | VrPm

Retirement | vrPM

PHASE ONE:
EARLY GROWTH

Infancy | VRpm

Old Age | vrpM

PHASE FIVE:
LATE AGING

Birth | Vrpm

Death | M

V: Vision/Leadership/Mission/Purpose/Core Values
R: Relationships/Experiences/Discipleship
P: Programmes/Events Ministries/Services/Activities
M: Management/Accountability/Systems/Resources

SETTING THE SCENE

The date 2 March 2014 will long be marked in the history of the local church I pastor. Six years before, we bought an imposing redundant Georgian church building, St. Mark's Church. A faith rollercoaster followed, with fundraising and renovation work totalling over £1 million.

Although the building has now become part of our story, we also felt part of the building's story. Following the British victory over Napoleon in the battle of Waterloo, a group of prominent Christians lobbied parliament to build churches in commemoration and thanksgiving. In 1818, parliament passed the Church Building Act, committing £1 million for the building of new churches, including St. Mark's, which was completed in 1825 at a cost of £9,637. In its heyday, the church family at St. Mark's was the heart of the community, with hundreds in attendance, and a separate church hall, day school, and row of almshouses. Sadly, the congregation dwindled through the latter part of the twentieth century, and a closing service was held in 2001.

But at our launch event on 2 March 2014, our fairly young congregation filled the space with worship again. We were celebrating, but we were also humbly aware that we were in part standing on the shoulders of the previous church life. The reality of this became increasingly apparent as we heard countless stories of schooling, weddings and funerals that had taken place in the building over the years.

WHAT'S THE BIG IDEA?

Although there are a handful of churches that can trace their history right back to the book of Acts, most experience a story of church death and new church life. The Life Cycle and Stages of Congregational Development diagram, created by church consultant George Bullard, follows a bell curve shape, plotting the journey of most living things – birth, growth, multiplication, plateau, decline and death – and applying it to a congregation.[22]

Ten suggested stages of a congregation's life are grouped into five phases:

Phase One: Early Growth involves the first five to seven years of the life of a congregation. It includes the stages of Birth and Infancy.

Phase Two: Late Growth involves ten to twelve years of the life of a congregation that carries it from about five to six years old to seventeen to eighteen years old. It includes the stages of Childhood and Adolescence.

Phase Three: Prime/Plateau involves seven to nine years of the life of a congregation. It includes the stages of Adulthood and Maturity, often including reproduction. This can be a stage where, because of the reproduction that has occurred, the church 'multiplies' by planting out or seeing new growth begin in other places.

Phase Four: Early Aging involves an indefinable number of years in the life of a congregation. It includes the stages of Empty Nest and Retirement.

Phase Five: Late Aging involves an indefinable number of years in the life of a congregation. It includes the Old Age and Death stages. This is not necessarily the end for the congregation, as it may go on to experience a new Life Cycle.

Each stage is assigned a combination of the letters VRPM, representing Vision, Relationships, Programmes and Management. These are capitalised when it is a likely dominant attribute at a particular stage in the Life Cycle. For example, Phase One is represented as Vrpm because Vision is a key element for this stage.

Although this is not a roadmap all congregations will follow, it helps set out a common cycle on which churches can plot their development, and can also facilitate meaningful and honest dialogue as to its pressing leadership needs. A church should aim to head towards, and remain in, the Adulthood phase, where Vision, Relationships, Programs and Management are all strong. (For churches that have reached Phase Three and beyond, this may mean moving backwards.) The Adulthood phase avoids 'business as usual'; a 'new vision' that disrupts the status quo may emerge, which prevents a decline.

THINKING BIBLICALLY

When it comes to the Life Cycle of churches, it's important to remember that God is sovereignly in control of their growth (1 Corinthians 3:6) and life (Revelation 2:5). It's interesting that throughout the whole of the New Testament letters, there is not one question answered, one prayer uttered or one encouragement offered about church numbers.

So, although our focus doesn't need to be on numbers, we do need to ensure our church life has strong Vision, Relationships, Programmes and Management. These four elements are evident in the New Testament church in Jerusalem.

Vision: The disciples know they are to 'make disciples' (Matthew 28:19), and so, empowered by the Spirit (Acts 2:4), they multiply (Acts 2:41). But their Vision doesn't end with their church family in Jerusalem; they send their best to see disciples made 'of all nations' (Matthew 28:19, Acts 11:22–27).

Relationships: The church culture was one of committed, sacrificial and sincere Relationships (Acts 2:42–47). When that was threatened, the leaders intervened (Acts 5:1–11).

Programmes: The church ensured that the widows among them were well looked after (Acts 6:1–7).

Management: The church had a valid concern over the intentions of the newly converted Paul, but the leadership structure ensured this situation was managed well (Acts 9:26–28).

HOW DO I APPLY IT?

No local church plans its own demise, but without consistent adaptation and change, decay and death can easily occur. Taking some time to humbly plot where your local church may be on the Life Cycle should raise questions as to what your church needs rights now.

A key moment in the cycle is when a church slips from the Adulthood to the Maturity phase, usually through a lack of Vision, where new initiatives that involve risk are avoided. Church members may feel, *We've worked hard to get here, and made many sacrifices; let's just enjoy what we have for a while.* A church can often avoid this trajectory by using its strength to invest in a new Vision, such as resourcing and releasing some of the congregation to plant a new church.

A strong Vision will empower people to forgo comfort and preference to see something wonderful emerge. Church leader and author Rick Warren says that 'Churches need more than just a once-a-year infusion of vision. They need constant reminders about what the church is all about.'[23] Indeed, churches with a clear mission and purpose are statistically more likely to grow.[24]

Although Vision is critical, without good Relationships, Programmes and Management, it won't get you very far. The following questions are helpful conversation starters:

Vision – Where should we go? i.e. What's the destination the Lord is calling your church to in one year, five years, ten years?

Relationships – Who should we bring? i.e. How connected is your church community and what will strengthen that?

Programmes – How will we get there? i.e. What sustainable rhythms of activity do we need to fulfil our Vision?

Management – What should we avoid? i.e. What structures need to be in place to ensure resilience?

QUESTIONS FOR REFLECTION

Where on the Life Cycle is your local church?

How strong are your church's Vision, Relationships, Programmes and Management?

What is the general and specific vision your local church has at the moment?

GO FURTHER

Read *The Purpose Driven Church* by Rick Warren.

We Are Family

DENOMINATION FAMILY TREE

ANDY

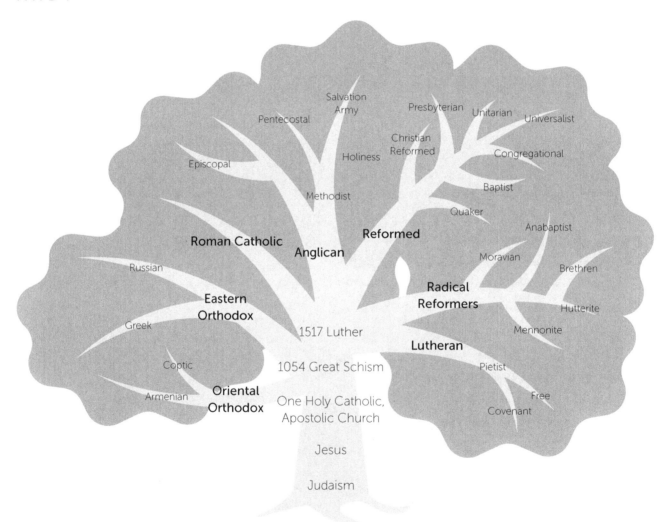

SETTING THE SCENE

If you've ever been to Egypt as a tourist, it's easy not to notice the persecution of Christians. There are some stunning church buildings where people go to worship, and Coptic priests wander the streets in their black gowns.

But behind the veneer of acceptance, many Christians are persecuted for their faith. When I went to Egypt, I visited the Coptic memorial for martyrs. This profound experience brought home the reality of some high-profile attacks, with personal items belonging to the martyrs giving a snapshot of their personality.

Some of these stories have hit our headlines, but much of the persecution that takes place in Egypt happens in the more everyday occurrences: when a bishop has to wait thirty years for permission to build a church building so that people can worship, or when a gospel meeting is denied a licence at the last minute, or when Christian women have their hair maliciously cut off while travelling on the metro.

At Christian conferences in the UK, we rarely hear from leaders of other Christian traditions. While I was in Egypt, I had the privilege of sitting with a Coptic priest and listening to his story of faith. He explained how martyrdom is a core part of the Bible colleges' syllabus. By contrast, in most Western Bible colleges, persecution would not get more than a passing mention in the syllabus. There is so much we can learn from other Christian traditions about what it means to follow Jesus.

WHAT'S THE BIG IDEA?

There are about 45,000 Christian denominations in the world today!

This Denomination Family Tree gives a snapshot of some of the major denominations and helps us see the origins of different branches. The diagram highlights seven major families of denominations, all of which are based on the birth, life, death and resurrection of Jesus. Each family of denominations splinters off into other denominations.

Following Judaism, Jesus and the establishment of the early church, we begin with a unified church (following Constantine's Nicene Creed) in the fourth century. This church is referred to as the 'One Holy Catholic Apostolic Church'. The first schism took place in the fifth century, mainly due to differing understandings of Jesus' divine and human nature. This first schism saw the Oriental Orthodox Church splinter off. The Oriental Orthodox family of denominations includes the Coptic Christians in Egypt, the Church of India, the Armenian Orthodox and the Ethiopian Orthodox Tewahedo Church.

Later, the Great Schism (1054) saw the Eastern Orthodox and the Roman Catholic Church emerge as distinctive denominations. The Eastern Orthodox Church had already become more independent from Rome, and various contentious issues and power plays came to a head when the Roman churches, without consulting the East, added to the Nicene Creed, inserting that the Holy Spirit proceeds from the Father 'and from the Son'. There was a big falling out, with Pope Leo IX excommunicating Michael Cerularius, the Patriarch of Constantinople, and the Patriarch retaliating by excommunicating Pope Leo IX.

Following this split, the Eastern Orthodox Church mainly consisted of the Greek and North African people groups and had a distinctly different culture of church governance to the Roman Catholic Church of the West.

The other four families of denominations are all Protestant and were formed as movements that wanted to reform the Roman Catholic Church. The Anglican split from Roman Catholicism was not primarily motivated by theological differences but involved a power-play by King Henry VIII to become 'Head of Church and State', dissolving all the Catholic monasteries in England, ensuring permission for his divorce and remarriage. Under Queen Elizabeth I, the Church of England was established with the aim of freeing England from the influence of foreign powers but with minimum confrontation. Most denominations have their roots in this family, including the Baptists, the Methodists and the many Pentecostal movements. The Radical Reformers are a strand of denominations that broke from Roman Catholicism before Luther's 95 Theses. The Lutheran Church was started by Martin Luther following his work that prompted the Reformation period. There have been few other significant denominations that have broken from this tradition.

While the Denominational Family Tree diagram doesn't perfectly represent the historical timeline, it does show the seven branches that have formed our main traditions in Christianity. And it helps us to remember that all of these denominations originated in Jesus.

THINKING BIBLICALLY

In Deuteronomy 12:1–14, God had spoken through Moses, prohibiting the building of altars other than those he had commanded. But the tribes on the east side of the Jordan River (Reuben, Gad and the half-tribe of Manasseh) had built an altar.

When the western tribes discovered this, they felt that God's Law had been violated. They were furious. Taking the commands in Deuteronomy 13:12–16 seriously, they were ready to destroy the tribes of Reuben, Gad and the half-tribe of Manasseh. From their point of view, Moses had not authorised the altar, and they suspected idolatry.

But before blood was shed, they investigated what had happened. And when they investigated, they discovered that the altar was actually a memorial to the Lord God. The eastern tribes explained that because they were geographically isolated from the rest of the nation, they had built the altar to show their connection. It was a sign of unity. When the western tribes understood where the eastern tribes were coming from, it helped heal the potential rift and civil war.

HOW DO I APPLY IT?

Over the years I have found this model useful in various contexts. Here are a few examples of where you might find it a helpful tool to share with those you lead:

- When people ask about your church community, this diagram can show where your stream of church fits into the grand scheme of church history. You could even use it as part of your church welcome overview.
- As you talk to people about what the many Christian traditions have in common, this diagram highlights that although there might be lots we disagree on, the Nicene Creed is core to what many of us believe.
- When explaining our differences, this diagram can help people understand why you hold a certain theological position. Tracing back down the tree can help people understand why you believe what you believe.
- When meeting those from other Christian streams, or exploring the use of certain traditions in our own settings, it can help bring understanding to some of the different perspectives and some of the roots of those beliefs and practices.
- Finally, I have found it helpful to critique some of the habits I have picked up over the years – some of the things I assumed were biblical are actually just cultural.

QUESTIONS FOR REFLECTION

How much does church history shape your church community today?

What are some of the prejudices you and your church may hold about other traditions? Have you explored them and tried to learn from other Christian denominational leaders?

What does this diagram reveal about humanity's understanding of and relationship with God and one another?

GO FURTHER

Read *Introduction to the History of Christianity*, 3rd ed. edited by Tim Dowley[25] and *Church History in Plain Language* by Bruce L. Shelley.[26]

Intentional and Relational

SNAKES AND LADDERS

ANDY

Committed Christian
and church member

Committed Christian but
no church connection

Lack of house groups
accessible to
shift-workers

BELIEVING

BELONGING

Faith exploring group

Agnostic church
attendee

Sympathetic to gospel but
no known Christian context

SETTING THE SCENE

As I previously mentioned, our family spent a year living in France – a year of croissants, strong cheese and re-learning French.

Although I'd spent years learning French at school and had managed to get a GCSE qualification, I'd never previously been in France for any length of time. Before we arrived, I revised lots of the words, brushing up my skills on Duolingo, and I felt confident speaking French when I practised on my own.

But although I'd learnt lots of vocabulary and grammar, getting to know people in France was an entirely different experience. There was the pronunciation, the speed at which people talked and the realisation that I had many gaps in my knowledge. On top of that, many people took the opportunity to practise their English with me, and so I never had a fully immersive experience.

Knowing the concepts as an individual was one thing, but without being immersed in community, I couldn't fully experience the language. My daughter, who was five at the time, had no French GCSE qualification before she arrived. She could barely say 'Bonjour'. Yet her experience of being fully immersed in a community of French speakers every day at school meant she had learnt the language within the year we were there.

WHAT'S THE BIG IDEA?

In evangelism circles, many will be familiar with the Engel scale, which charts the faith journey – from no knowledge of God, through to spiritual maturity as a Christian. But the danger is we often think of a person's spiritual journey in isolation from their journey into community.

Evangelist Marcus Bennett's model, Snakes and Ladders, helps us map out both of those journeys – the journey of Believing and the journey of Belonging and how they work together. This model helps us consider how someone can explore faith as they discover what it means to become part of a Christian community.[27] He writes:

As we look to make disciples, people need two things. Firstly, they need knowledge about Jesus and an understanding of the Gospel but secondly, they need relationships with Christians and the church community. Jesus commissions us to make disciples. We are wanting to help people make more than just a momentary decision to pray a prayer. We are wanting to help them become followers of Jesus who understand what it means to be part of God's family, the Church.

The horizontal axis on the model shows the relational connectivity of an individual as they meet with Christians through church activities, such as a social action project – labelled 'Belonging'. The far left shows no known connection to Christians or the church, and the far right shows a deep connection and belonging to the church.

The vertical axis represents a person's understanding and response to the Christian faith – labelled 'Believing'. The bottom of the axis would represent a person with no understanding or interest in the gospel, and the top of the axis would indicate a mature, passionate Christian.

Where the two axes cross (zero) is the point where an individual decides to follow Jesus and feels like they belong to the church community.

The model is called Snakes and Ladders, based on the children's game, because it gives us two distinct challenges. First, it begs the question: How are we building ladders for people to journey in faith and to find their home in the church? Second, it challenges us with the question: What are the snakes that are working against people coming closer to faith and to belonging to the church community? Possible snakes could be cliques in the church that are unwelcoming, a lack of childcare provision or a church culture that doesn't relate to where the person is at.

THINKING BIBLICALLY

When we look at how Jesus taught his disciples, he didn't simply give them a learning experience in a classroom setting. Their belief in who Jesus was grew as they experienced life with him, in community.

As the disciples journeyed together, they must have experienced a deep sense of belonging. And it is during these times together that the disciples had moments of believing about who Jesus is, for example, when the disciples say, 'What kind of man is this? Even the winds and the waves obey him!' (Matthew 8:27).

Jesus was intentional in helping the disciples grow in both their believing and their belonging. He taught them about God's Kingdom, but he was also deeply relational, eating with the disciples and including them in his ministry. As we invite others to explore the Christian faith, they will need help to not only grow in their believing but also to grow in their sense of belonging and living out faith with others in community.

HOW DO I APPLY IT?

Draw the matrix on a large piece of paper and plot the activities you run as a church.

For example, the parent and toddler group may connect with those outside of the church community, giving a great sense of belonging, but may have little faith content. This would be in the bottom right quadrant. An online Bible training course may be for those who are already committed Christians to take them deeper in their biblical understanding, but it doesn't help them grow in relationship with other Christians due to the remote access learning style. This would be in the upper left quadrant.

Once you have plotted these activities, think about how they could become ladders that help people on the journey to increased believing or belonging. You might want to introduce a Bible story segment to your toddler group, or run an Alpha course that you could invite parents to over lunch after the session. You could create an online connection time for the Bible Study course, so that participants can meet one another and share how their learning is going.

You can also think about what gaps there are across the life of your church. Is there a suitable and coherent path for a journey from the bottom left quadrant to the upper right? What can you tweak, or where can you start to fill those gaps?

If you are feeling brave, you can add the snakes. If you're honest, what is causing people to slip away from feeling relationally connected or growing spiritually? What could you do to tackle these challenges?

QUESTIONS FOR REFLECTION

Where would you plot those in the wider community, who aren't connected to the church, but who you are journeying with?

Are there opportunities for them to connect with the church community to grow in their sense of belonging?

Who is connected with the church community but doesn't have much spiritual connection? What might you be able to offer them to invite them further on that journey?

GO FURTHER

Watch Marcus Bennett speak about the Snakes and Ladders diagram at youtube.com/watch?v=hxGYKxJuax0.

49

Considering Relevance

THE CONTEXTUALISATION STAIRCASE
CHRIS

Levels of a Church's Contextual Approach (C)	C1	C2	C3	C4	C5	C6
Church's Self-Description	Our church is purposefully separated from culture.	Our church is foreign to the local community in both culture and language.	Our church understands the culture and makes concessions for it.	Our church is using cultural elements that are relevant to the people we are reaching.	Our church is using cultural elements but is distanced from organised Christian community.	We effectively operate as secret believers.
Locals' Perception of the Church	A religious group, where I am not welcome.	A church where I am welcome, but I don't understand what's happening.	A church where I am welcome, and I can join in.	A group with people like me who have Christian beliefs and practices.	A group where I am welcome with some spiritual beliefs and practices.	A group I am unaware exists or I have assumed is a social group.

SETTING THE SCENE

In September 1853, a small three-masted clipper slipped quietly out of Liverpool harbour. Aboard was Hudson Taylor, a gaunt and wild-eyed twenty-one-year-old missionary. He was headed for a country that was just coming into the Christian West's consciousness, with only a few dozen missionaries stationed there.

In the years before he moved to China, Taylor prepared by learning the rudiments of medicine, studying Mandarin and immersing himself ever deeper in the Bible and prayer.

Upon landing in China, Taylor made a radical decision, at least for Protestant missionaries of the day: He decided to dress in Chinese clothes and grow a pigtail (as Chinese men did). His fellow Protestants were either incredulous or critical. By the time Taylor died, a half-century later, China was viewed as the most fertile and challenging of mission fields, with thousands volunteering annually to serve there.

Taylor consciously chose to contextually relate to the people he sought to reach. In the same way, our churches also need to consider our contextual approach.

WHAT'S THE BIG IDEA?

Although the gospel never changes, how churches present the gospel does – at least to some degree. Whether they are aware of it or not, every church has a philosophy of contextualisation. That philosophy will be outworked, positively or negatively, in the way your church relates to its context.

This philosophy affects the language we use, the clothes we wear and how we spend time together. More specifically, it influences how we communicate the good news of Jesus. For example, there is a growing awareness of the difference between shame and guilt cultures and the need to highlight the benefits of the gospel accordingly. This all relates to the Snakes and Ladders diagram (page 210); cultural connection can create ladders into church life, whereas cultural disconnection can create snakes away from church life.

The Contextualisation Staircase helps you assess your contextual approach and can spark conversation and debate as to whether it's the right one. It's based upon the 'C1 to C6 spectrum'.[28]

THINKING BIBLICALLY

Paul contextualises his message masterfully in Acts 17. He begins by observing the culture around him as he 'walked around and looked carefully' (verse 23) at the idols in Athens. He uses these observations to build bridges: "'I see that in every way you are very religious'" (verse 22). One Methodist minister, commenting on this passage, said, 'Make no mistake, today's equivalent is a Methodist minister walking into a witch's coven and declaiming, "I see we share an interest in spiritual things."'[29] As part of his gospel proclamation, Paul then goes on to quote two contemporary, culturally popular philosophers (Acts 17:22–28).

Paul demonstrates not only how to read and relate to culture, but also how to confront it. He was 'greatly distressed to see that the city was full of idols' (verse 16) and went on to challenge 'all people everywhere to repent. For [God] has set a day when he will judge the world' (verse 31).

Clearly Paul was willing to adapt in relevant ways to reach people, but he never changed the core gospel content (Galatians 1:8).

HOW DO I APPLY IT?

In our world today, there is an increased polarisation in opinions and lifestyle choices. So it's important that we discover ways to reach across cultural divides, connect with others and demonstrate God's love in a meaningful way. After all, Jesus' good news to the world is that we should love our neighbour as ourselves.

As you think about the approaches in the diagram, consider who God has called you to love and serve.

The ideal step for a church to be situated is C4, where 'outsiders' are more likely to feel welcomed and connected, while also being aware of the gospel-centrality of the church community.

If you think your church fits the C1, C2 or C3 descriptions, you may want to consider how you could be more effective in connecting with those outside the church. By somewhat distancing yourself from the culture, can you constructively relate to it or serve the people of that culture? Where might your understanding of a particular culture help you to relate to the people within it? Where are the similarities and overlaps that might help you find common ground?

Could your church be providing culturally appropriate bridges for guests, such as Halal meat at community meals or shifting your service times to avoid clashes with major sports fixtures? If you're reaching out to young people, do you need to listen to and learn about the music they love so that you can understand their passion? If you're welcoming those who aren't Bible literate into your services, could you provide Bibles in the seats and use the page number references, rather than book, chapter and verse, so that they know where to find the passage?

If you'd categorise your church in the C5 or C6 descriptions, you may want to consider whether you're being as countercultural as you should be. Western cultural idols are more subversive and pervasive than they were in Athens. Think about our football stadiums with signs that read, 'This is where we worship'[30] or the shopping malls designed like temples,[31] where we rush for retail therapy. Are you 'greatly distressed' (Acts 17:16) at the idols you see, recognising that they seek to steal our time, money, energy and affection with false promises of satisfying the God-ache in our hearts?

Perhaps we need to consider whether our own church culture engages too much with the idols of our society rather than focusing on becoming the Christ-centred communities we are created to be. Are we encouraging a culture of performance in our church services, placing too much emphasis on the way we dress? Or are we inadvertently promoting an unhealthy work-life balance by the way we operate our ministries?

As churches, we are seeking to love the people we're reaching by pointing them to the good news of Jesus. Pastor and author Timothy Keller says we should be 'giving people the Bible's answers, which they may not at all want to hear, to questions about life that people in their particular time and place are asking, in language and forms they can comprehend, and through appeals and arguments with force they can feel, even if they reject them'.[32]

QUESTIONS FOR REFLECTION

Which level of contextual approach best describes your church?

How might you do a 'culture assessment' of the people-group(s) you are reaching out to?

How willing are you to change the way you operate church life in order to make others feel welcomed?

GO FURTHER

Read *A Non-Anxious Presence* by Mark Sayers.[33]

Knowing the Next Step

THE 5PS

ANDY

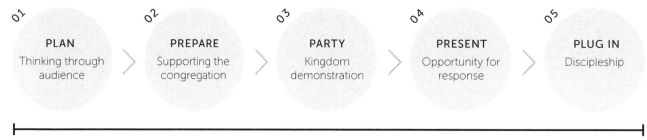

01
PLAN
Thinking through
audience

02
PREPARE
Supporting the
congregation

03
PARTY
Kingdom
demonstration

04
PRESENT
Opportunity for
response

05
PLUG IN
Discipleship

RELATIONSHIPS & PRAYER

SETTING THE SCENE

In twenty years supporting churches in sharing Jesus, I have experienced all kinds of outreach activities – some that have worked brilliantly and some less so!

Once I attended a church fun day, with bouncy castles and a barbecue. It was a great celebration in the community, but all the Christians at the event were so busy cooking burgers and carrying out health and safety checks that there was little time for guest interaction or gospel conversations. Many of the guests didn't even realise it was the church that had hosted the event.

Another time I was invited to speak at an evening event and had been told to expect many unchurched people, but when I arrived, I was asked, somewhat apologetically, to change my message because everyone present was already a Christian.

From these experiences, I have become convinced that the church needs to be more intentional as we look to give people opportunities to explore the Christian faith.

WHAT'S THE BIG IDEA?

Jesus came proclaiming the Kingdom in all kinds of different settings. He shared the good news with the crowds and with individuals. People turned and followed him through the bigger events as well as through smaller, relational settings. As churches seeking to share the message of God's Kingdom with the people around us, we need to have a mixture of approaches where we both 'go' to people and invite people to 'come' to us. The 5Ps is a simple framework to help churches think through how they are sharing Jesus in the community.

Plan: Start by creating a mission team who will take responsibility for the prayerful planning of the 5Ps. Explore what God is already doing in your community and identify where you are being called to focus your evangelism in this season. Consider who you are reaching and what their needs and desires might be. For example, we once ran a community fashion show, working with local charity shops to promote ethical clothing. This resonated with local people in the area who were passionate about this issue and provided local families with more sustainable and affordable clothing.

By understanding who we are called to reach, we can think through how the gospel relates to them. This might mean your event doesn't happen in a church building but in a school hall or community centre, where people might feel more comfortable. The point isn't getting people in the church building; it's about connecting with the people in the community.

Prepare: This is about helping the wider congregation understand the mission strategy, to know what's planned and to prepare. The event may be led by a smaller team within the church, but it's vital that the whole congregation knows what's happening and what to expect.

Many Christians can be wary of inviting their friends to church events when they are not sure what's happening. By explaining what will happen at the event and what the desired outcome is, we can allay fears and encourage people to make personal invitations.

Preparation involves upskilling the congregation on sharing their faith and having more faith conversations so that they can articulate why they follow Jesus.

Party: These events are an opportunity to represent the values of Christ; to find out that the church isn't overly weird and that God is good. This is about hosting a party that puts the church at the heart of the community and demonstrates Kingdom values.

You might hold a film evening or a curry night. You might choose a community banquet or invite people to join a choir event. This is not an opportunity to preach a thirty-minute sermon! In fact, unless we specify there is going to be a talk, there shouldn't be one. But we can let people know how to find out more – this is basically an invitation to a Present event.

Present: This an opportunity for people who have connected with the church to hear a gospel presentation. It could be a special church service, or a guest speaker sharing over a meal, or even somebody from the church doing a Bible study over coffee. The important thing is that people are given an opportunity to make some kind of response. That response could be to become a Christian or to explore more of the Christian faith by reading one of the Gospels or by doing a course that further introduces Christianity.

Plug in: This is a discipleship-based programme that helps people who want to make a commitment get to grips with the gospel and plug in to the local church. The biggest mistake we can make in creating a missional strategy is not expecting people to come to faith! We should think through this fifth P from the very beginning of the 5Ps process.

These 5Ps act as building blocks to think through what mission looks like as a local church. However, all of this will be completely ineffective if we don't underpin everything with the two vital ingredients of prayer and relationships.

THINKING BIBLICALLY

We tend to think that people either come to faith in Jesus or reject him on their first encounter. However, the story of the Pharisee Nicodemus demonstrates that for some people there is a journey.

Nicodemus had heard about Jesus and was obviously intrigued because in John 3 he meets with him under the cover of night. Jesus challenges him that he must be 'born again' (John 3:3), but it seems he doesn't make a commitment there and then.

Some time later, as plans are hatched to arrest Jesus, Nicodemus bravely declares that Jesus must be heard out. He says, "'Does our law judge a man without first giving him a hearing and learning what he does?'" (John 7:51 ESV). He is willing to speak out for what is right, despite the animosity towards Jesus.

The final time we hear of Nicodemus is in John 19, after Jesus' crucifixion. Here, he isn't afraid of honouring Jesus despite the fact Jesus has just been executed. He helps Joseph of Arimathea with Jesus' burial, generously bringing seventy-five pounds of spices.

For Nicodemus there was connection, there was conversation and, ultimately, there was an opportunity for him to show his commitment. The stepping stones in his faith journey remind us to make sure we're creating opportunities for those we're reaching out to.

HOW DO I APPLY IT?

Gather a team to begin the process. The first and most important question to ask together is: *What is God doing in our community?* As you discuss, write down how your church is already connected with the community.

Once you have prayerfully discerned what God is doing in your community and who you want to intentionally connect with, think through each of the Ps. How will you Plan to share the vision and Prepare your congregation to share Jesus with them? What kind of Party events do you already do in the community, or what new events could you create?

What kind of Present event would fit best for those who are interested? And do you have a Plug in? Discipleship takes an investment of time, prayer and energy and may require shifts in how we do church with new expressions that connect with those who have decided they want to follow Jesus. What will a discipleship journey look like for a new Christian?

QUESTIONS FOR REFLECTION

As a church, do you have a strategy to reach your community through events?

Which of the 5Ps might be the most challenging for your church? How might you be strategic in ensuring this isn't a weak link in the process?

Who in your church could be key for helping you to adopt this strategy?

GO FURTHER

Read *5Ps of Mission Development and How to Get Started* by Andy Frost at sharejesusinternational.com/5Ps.

Kingdom Transformation

FOUR RELATIONSHIPS

CHRIS

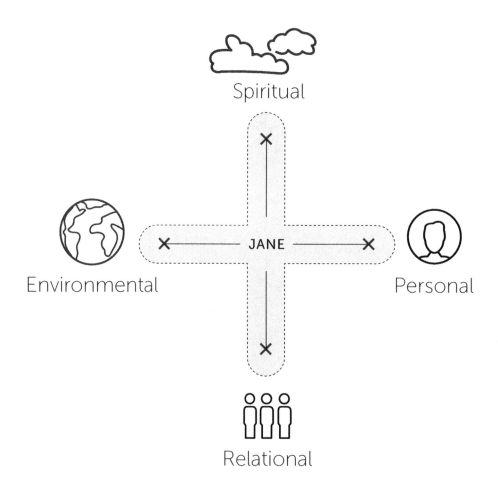

SETTING THE SCENE

In 2008, police in Frankfurt discovered a huge stash of unopened mail in a postman's home, stored in sacks, boxes and under his mattress. Police were alerted after a neighbour spotted him trying to dispose of the mail in the rubbish.

The postman had failed to deliver over 20,000 letters and parcels because of the demands of his part-time studies. It had got to the point that he felt too overwhelmed to catch up. Two vans were required to remove the mail, which police said he had been collecting since August 2007. There was even post addressed to the man himself. 'The 23-year-old had not opened any of the letters but simply stored them so he would not have to deliver them,' a local police statement said. The postman faced charges of theft and misappropriation of mail.[34]

Just like the postman, are our churches hoarding the good news of Jesus? Are we equipping people to be confident in knowing and communicating this message of good news, so that they don't feel overwhelmed and fail to deliver it?

WHAT'S THE BIG IDEA?

Over the years, several popular diagrams have emerged to help explain the gospel, such as the Bridge to Life and the Roman Road. But these tools can fail to express the enormity of the gospel and how good the news about Jesus really is.

The Four Relationships diagram illustrates how our whole lives are transformed by this good news – that Jesus' death and resurrection has enabled his rule and reign on earth, not only restoring our relationship with God but also renewing our identities, our relationships with one another and our care for the world around us.

THINKING BIBLICALLY

We can often feel intimidated or unsure about how to share the good news of Jesus with those around us, but Isaiah 52:7 reminds us that there is something beautiful in being the bearers of this message: 'How beautiful on the mountains are the feet of those who bring good news . . .'.

If we're going to share this message, it's important that we know what's so special about it. When Jesus came proclaiming, 'The Kingdom of God has come' (Mark 1:15), he wasn't just referring to life after death; he came announcing a new rule and reign for the people on earth.

If we consider who rules and reigns in our world today, it can be pretty disheartening. We see dictatorships or corrupted leaders. We see the rich exploiting the poor. We see strength expressed through the violent oppression of the vulnerable, and the ruin of the natural world for selfish gain.

But Jesus came to reign in a different way – with an upside-down kind of Kingdom. His Kingdom brings blessing to the poor in spirit, comfort to those in mourning, and reward for the meek (Matthew 5:3–5). Jesus' reign didn't come about through earthly means of power but through sacrifice. His leadership was servant-hearted, and he calls those who follow him to lay down their lives (John 13:37).

So, the good news of this new Kingdom is not only about eternal life but also about our transformed life, here on earth. God's Kingdom reign enables a restored relationship with him (Romans 6:23), but it also works to reconcile all aspects of life (Colossians 1:19–20). As Kingdom citizens, God is working with us to begin redeeming our self-identity (2 Corinthians 3:18), our relationships (John 13:34–35) and the environment (Genesis 1:28).

HOW DO I APPLY IT?

The Four Relationships diagram helps us paint a picture of what God's rule and reign can look like in our lives. This is a tool you could teach those in your church to use when someone they know is open to hearing the gospel. Some people will find it helpful to actually draw it, whereas others might find it a useful mental image to guide them as they have conversations about faith.

Using a piece of paper and pen, follow this seven-step process:

1. Write the listener's name in the middle of the paper, e.g., Jane, and suggest that Jane may well be asking four central questions throughout her life.

2. Draw a mirror to the right of Jane and a connecting line, and suggest the first question may be, 'How do I relate to myself?' This is the Personal question.

3. Draw a group of people below Jane and a connecting line, and suggest the second question may be, 'How do I relate to other people?' This is the Relational question.

4. Draw an image of the world and a connecting line to the left of Jane, and suggest the third question may be, 'How do I relate to the planet?' This is the Environmental question.

5. Draw a cloud above Jane with a connecting line, and suggest the fourth question may be, 'How do I relate to God?' Perhaps even, 'Does God exist?' This is the Spiritual question.

6. As you draw Xs towards the ends of the four lines, explain how the Bible teaches that all of these relationships have been broken by our sin or selfishness. So, in our relationship with ourselves, we tend to either be self-centred or full of self-hatred. Our relationships with others end through division or death. Our relationship with the planet has triggered a ticking time bomb of climate change. But, most significantly, our relationship with God has been broken. (You may like to unpack these ideas with personal stories or Scripture.)

7. As you draw the shape of a cross around the four lines, you can express how the Bible teaches that God loves Jane so much that he came as Jesus, first and foremost to offer her a path back into the right relationship with him. Explain that Jesus did this by dying on a cross, where he took on the full cost of her sin but then rose victoriously three days later and ascended to heaven. Finish by saying that once her relationship with God has been restored, he will show her how to have better relationships with herself, others and the planet. (Again, you may like to unpack these ideas with personal stories or Scripture.)

This diagram can also be used to consider how your church life is equipping individuals to see personal, relational, environmental and spiritual transformation.

QUESTIONS FOR REFLECTION

How does the idea of the gospel affecting these four areas of life impact your view of sharing the good news?

How might you equip yourself to feel confident in using this tool?

How might you equip your church with this tool?

Are there pathways in your church life for people to see transformation in the personal, relational and environmental aspects of their life?

GO FURTHER

Watch the Bible Project talk about the meaning of the word 'gospel' at youtube.com/watch?v=HT41M013X3A.

Watch 'Changing church for climate justice' at vimeo.com/622750015.

Watch the Bible Project talk about how the good news is more than just eternal life after death at youtube.com/watch?v=uCOyclMyJZM.

Unity for Transformation

THE GATHER MOVEMENT MODEL
ANDY

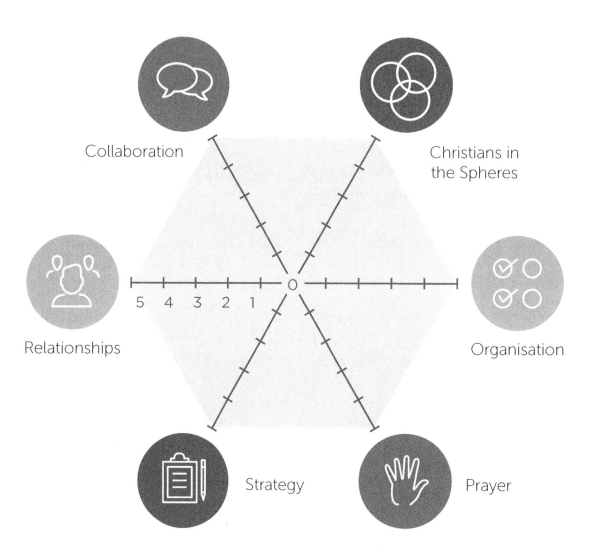

SETTING THE SCENE

Many Christians were sceptical about the idea of a large-scale arts festival celebrating the Christian faith in the heart of London. Though a relatively small charity, Share Jesus International had a big vision: to take the church outside its four walls and put the festival of Pentecost back on the map. But to fulfil it would require a whole swathe of London churches to commit to unity, which, given past history, seemed impossible. Yet the vision was compelling enough to drive that dream. Most of the events would be free, bringing the broad spectrum of churches across the capital together in glorious unity. With one voice, Pentecost could be celebrated like never before.

Christian charities and churches saw the beauty of partnership. They laid down their brands. They invested financially, and their differences became their strength. From 2008 to 2012, the vision of Pentecost Festival became a reality in the heart of London. In each of the five years it ran, an average of one hundred unique events took place in over eighty venues, enabling 30,000 Londoners and tourists to discover what Pentecost is all about.

The programme was broad, ranging from film premieres in Leicester Square to hip-hop performances in parks and biblical performances in West End theatres. There were comedy nights in swanky bars, prominent scientists explaining faith in university lecture halls and young people campaigning for justice on the streets. Worship times were held in large auditoriums, gospel choirs sang on the streets and prayers were offered in Trafalgar Square.

Local churches helped to distribute 100,000 printed programmes, inviting people to discover that church is not just a place to go on Sunday morning but is also about God's people bringing hope to the world. The festival captured the imagination of the press, with a live broadcast on BBC One, interviews on Radio 4 and listings in *Time Out*. Church was visible, and the power of a united church spoke into society.

For sure, Pentecost Festival was riding on a wave of God's grace, but it shows what can be achieved when churches and Christian charities work together. In 2012, we packaged up the experiences into a festival guide and trained eighty church unity groups in this model of mission. Many of these annual festivals continue to this day.

WHAT'S THE BIG IDEA?

We can often think that church unity is an annual joint church service or a church leaders' breakfast once a term, but when we look beyond our local churches and think about how we pastor our communities, it becomes evident that we have to work together. In my work with a charity called Gather Movement, we have devised this model that helps maximise potential impact through church unity in a town or city. The model focuses on six key areas.

- **Collaboration**. The church works in collaboration with civic authorities, charity leaders, sphere leaders and prayer leaders.

- **Relationships**. Christian leaders are in close, accountable, trusting relationships with each other.

- **Organisation**. There is a regular rhythm of meeting, a clear structure, a core team and well-managed finances.

- **Prayer**. There is coordinated and passionate town/city prayer.

- **Strategy**. There is a long-term strategic plan for the Kingdom to come, involving evangelism and social impact at a town/city-wide level.

- **Christians in the Spheres**. Different spheres of your town/city – health, education, business, charity – reflect Christian unity. For example, the Pentecost Festival mentioned above touched on many different spheres, but as leaders you might show unity in a business setting or in a hospital or school.

THINKING BIBLICALLY

Psalm 133 begins with the words, 'How good and pleasant it is when God's people live together in unity!' This psalm, written by King David, is one of the 'psalms of ascent' that was sung as pilgrims ascended the road to Jerusalem to attend festivals. It would have been sung as people from across the nation gathered on their pilgrimage – young and old, rich and poor – reminding them that they were family.

One of the pictures the Psalms gives us of this unity is through the image of oil running down Aaron's beard. Oil was refreshing in the dry and dusty climate. And this was not just any oil but precious oil, suitable for anointing a priest (Exodus 30:22–33). It was poured in abundance, running from the head, through the beard and down onto the collar of Aaron's robes. As High Priest, Aaron would have had a robe with the names of the twelve tribes of Israel sewn into it (Exodus 28:12). The image here is of the oil cascading down, bringing refreshment on the people of God.

Throughout Scripture, there is a call for God's people to be one. In Jesus' prayer in John 17, he beautifully calls us to be one so that the world will know that God sent Jesus and that God loves the world (John 17:20–26).

HOW DO I APPLY IT?

If you already have an existing church unity group, then this diagram can be printed off next time you gather. Ask each leader to make a mark on the six areas, from 1 to 5, for how well your church unity group is engaging in each area. Once everyone has filled their diagram in, ask people to share where they rated the unity group and why. Use this as an exercise to explore where God might be calling you to develop in the next season. You can't focus on every area at once!

If there is no existing church unity group in your area, why not try to start one! Many of them start around gathering leaders together relationally, but it might be that you start a group by collaborating with civic leaders to find out what the needs are in your community and how the church collectively may be able to play a role.

QUESTIONS FOR REFLECTION

How great an impact can your church make in your town or city? How much greater could this impact be if you worked more closely with other churches and organisations?

How much time do you spend building inter-church relationships?

What stops you from working more with other churches? How might you get over some of those hurdles?

GO FURTHER

For lots of resources around this, check out gathermovement.org.

ACKNOWLEDGEMENTS

Thank you to the trustees of Share Jesus International for believing in this project, and to Gateway Church, Leeds for gifting Chris a sabbatical, when he wrote much of his content.

Thank you to everyone who helped put the puzzle pieces of *Leadiagrams* together, especially 100 Movements Publishing, Helen Bearn, Anna Robinson, Daniel Watson Design and Lucy Coates; your diligence and skill has been so incredibly helpful. Thank you, as well, to the leadership experts who graciously gave us permission to use their diagrams.

Also, a big thank you to our wives, both called Jo, who are outstanding leaders themselves; for their regular input and patience as we talked about little but diagrams for over a year!

Notes

SECTION 1: LEADING YOURSELF

1   George Müller, *A Narrative of Some of the Lord's Dealings with George Mueller* (Dust and Ashes Publications, 2003), 730–732.

2   Trevor Hudson, *The Cycle of Grace: Living in Sacred Balance* (Upper Room Books, 2013).

3   Gary L. Thomas, *Sacred Pathways: Discover Your Soul's Path to God* (Zondervan, 2002).

4   See studylight.org/commentaries/eng/bnb/psalms-100.html.

5   Albert Hibbert, *Smith Wigglesworth: The Secret of His Power* (Harrison House Publishers, 2009), p.32.

6   Tony Schwartz, *The Way We're Working Isn't Working: The Four Forgotten Needs That Energize Great Performance* (Simon & Schuster, 2016).

7   Tony Schwartz, *Be Excellent at Anything* (Simon & Schuster, 2011), p.xii.

8   Joseph Luft, *Of Human Interaction: The Johari Model* (Mayfield Publishing Company, 1969).

9   Maury Peiperl, 'Getting 360-Degree Feedback Right', *Harvard Business Review*, January 2001, hbr.org/2001/01/getting-360-degree-feedback-right.

10 Peter Scazzero, *The Emotionally Healthy Leader* (Zondervan, 2015).

11 Robert Plutchik and Henry Kellerman (eds), *Emotion: Theory, Research, and Experience: Vol. 1. Theories of Emotion* (Academic Press, 1990).

12 Charles Spurgeon, 'Joy and Peace in Believing', *The Metropolitan Tabernacle Pulpit* (MTP), Vol. 12, Sermon 692, spurgeongems.org/vols10-12/chs692.pdf.

13 Addressing the Questions of Every Decade, emotionallyhealthy.org/addressing-the-questions-of-every-decade.

14 Rob Frost, Destiny: *A Journey Across Three Generations with Rob Frost* (Authentic Media, 2003).

15 Vaughan Roberts, *True Friendship* (10Publishing, 2013).

16 John Mark Comer, *The Ruthless Elimination of Hurry: How to Stay Emotionally Healthy and Spiritually Alive in the Chaos of the Modern World* (Hodder & Stoughton, 2019).

17 Brian Tracy, *Master Your Time, Master Your Life* (Tarcherperigee, 2017).

18 Kevin Macdonald, *Touching the Void*, 23 January 2004, USA.

19 Peter, along with other Scripture writers, consistently emphasises our new identity in Christ to save us from adopting alternative identities founded in roots such as the unique pressures we face.

20 John Piper, 'None of Our Misery Is Meaningless', *Desiring God*, 9 July 2018, desiringgod.org/messages/the-glory-of-god-in-the-sight-of-eternity/excerpts/none-of-our-misery-is-meaningless.

21 Virginia Huguenot, 'Cellar of Affliction', *Virginia is for Huguenots*, 25 August 2009, virginiahuguenot.blogspot.com/2009/08/cellar-of-affliction.html..

22 Karl Pillemer, *30 Lessons for Living: Tried and True Advice from the Wisest Americans* (Avery Publishing, 2012).

23 Jim Collins, *Good to Great* (Random House Business, 2001).

SECTION 2: LEADING OTHERS

1   Elisabeth Kübler-Ross, *On Death and Dying* (Macmillan, 1969).

2   Elisabeth Kübler-Ross and David Kessler, *On Grief and Grieving: Finding the Meaning of Grief Through the Five Stages of Loss* (Simon & Schuster, 2005).

3   Kate Murphy, *You're Not Listening: What You're Missing and Why It Matters* (Vintage, 2021).

4   Stephen B. Karpman, M.D., *A Game Free Life. The definitive book on the Drama Triangle and Compassion Triangle by the originator and author. The new transactional analysis of intimacy, openness, and happiness* (Drama Triangle Publications, 2014).

5   Stephen Covey, *The 7 Habits of Highly Effective People* (Free Press, 1989).

6   Kerry Patterson, *Crucial Conversations: Tools for Talking When Stakes are High,* 2nd ed. (McGraw Hill, 2011).

7   Albert Mehrabian, *Silent Messages: Implicit Communication of Emotions and Attitudes* (Wadsworth Publishing Company, 1981).

8   Kenneth Wayne Thomas, *Thomas-Kilmann Conflict Mode Instrument* (CPP, Inc., 2002).

9   Jordan Peterson, *12 Rules for Life: An Antidote to Chaos* (Penguin, 2019).

10   Bruce W. Tuckman, 'Developmental Sequence in Small Groups', *Psychology Bulletin* (1965), pubmed.ncbi.nlm.nih.gov/14314073.

11   Donald B. Egolf, *Forming Storming Norming Performing: Successful Communication in Groups and Teams* (iUniverse, 2001).

12   'Boris Johnson resignation: Sajid Javid says prayer meeting moved him to quit', BBC News, 10 July 2022, bbc.co.uk/news/uk-politics-62113401.

13   For example, in blaming Simon Case for allowing 'a drinking culture to develop into rule-breaking parties'. Toby Helm, 'Boris Johnson to sacrifice top official over Partygate to save himself', The Observer, 21 May 2002, theguardian.com/politics/2022/may/21/boris-johnson-to-sacrifice-top-official-over-partygate-to-save-himself.

14   'Five Dysfunctions of a Team by Patrick Lencioni', youtube.com/watch?v=GCxct4CR-To.

15   Patrick M. Lencioni, *The Five Dysfunctions of a Team: A Leadership Fable* (John Wiley & Sons, 2002).

16   Patrick Lencioni, *The Ideal Team Player: How to Recognize and Cultivate the Three Essential Virtues* (Jossey-Bass, 2016).

17   'Leadership and Followership: What Tango Teaches Us About These Roles in Life', 2011, youtube.com/watch?v=Cswrnc1dggg.

18   Robert E. Kelley, *The Power of Followership: How to Create Leaders People Want to Follow and Followers Who Lead Themselves* (Bantam Dell Publishing Group, 1992).

19   Adidas Football, 'Never Follow Feat. Paul Pogba' (2016), youtube.com/watch?v=kKRmbS_b250.

20   For example, Challeff's tool here: courageousfollower.net/followership-books/the-courageous-follower-self-assessment-of-your-followership-style.

21   Paul Hersey, Kenneth H. Blanchard, *Management of Organizational Behavior: Utilizing Human Resources* (Prentice Hall, 1972).

SECTION 3: LEADING PROJECTS

1   See axelrodgroup.com/meeting-canoe.

2   Phillip Clampitt, Robert DeKoch, Thomas Cashman, 'A Strategy for communicating about uncertainty', *The Academy of Management Executive*, November 2000: 41.

3   Ibid.

4   Address at the Second Assembly of the World Council of Churches, Evanston, Illinois, August 19 1954, presidency.ucsb.edu/documents/address-the-second-assembly-the-world-council-churches-evanston-illinois.

5   Stephen Covey, *The 7 Habits of Highly Effective People*, reprinted edition (Simon & Schuster, 2017).

6   Aesop's Fables, *The Hare and the Tortoise*, taken from fablesofaesop.com/the-hare-and-the-tortoise.html.

7   Daniel Kahneman, *Thinking, Fast and Slow* (Penguin, 2012).

8   Ibid., p. 20.

9   Ibid., p. 20.

10   Ibid., p. 3.

11   Daniel Kahneman, Jack Knetsch and Richard Thaler, 'Anomalies: The Endowment Effect, Loss Aversion, and Status Quo Bias', *The Journal of Economic Perspectives*, Vol. 5 (1), 1991, pp. 193–206.

12   John P. Kotter, 'Leading change', *Harvard Business Review Press* (2012).

13   See Gerry Johnson, Richard Whittington, Kevan Scholes, et al. *Exploring strategy: text and cases*, 11th ed. (Pearson, 2017), p. 460.

14   Nehemiah isn't the real hero of the story, as the text points us towards the coming of Jesus. Where Nehemiah's vision for the walls caused him to weep over Jerusalem (Nehemiah 1:4), Jesus' vision for his people also caused him to weep over Jerusalem (Luke 19:41). Where Nehemiah left the comfort and safety of the palace (Nehemiah 2:9), Jesus left the comfort and safety of heaven (John 1:14). And where Nehemiah had a plot on his life to kill him (Nehemiah 6:2), Jesus was actually killed (Luke 23:46).

15   John P. Kotter, 'Accelerate: Building Strategic Agility for a Faster-Moving World', *Harvard Business Review*, April 2014, hbr.org/2014/04/accelerate-building-strategic-agility-for-a-faster-moving-world.

16   Richard P. Francisco, 'Five Levels of Interpersonal Communication: A Model that Works Across Cultures', *Learning with Experience*, learningwithexperience.com/uploads/1/2/0/7/120775390/five_levels__of_interpersonal_communication_-_francisco.pdf.

17   John Powell, *Why Am I Afraid to Tell You Who I Am?* (Fount, 1999).

18   Woody Wade, *Scenario Planning: A Field Guide for the Future* (Wiley, 2012).

19   Max Bazerman and Margaret Neale, 'Nonrational escalation of commitment in negotiation', *European Management Journal*, 10, no. 2 (1992): 163–68.

20   Roger Fisher and William Ury, *Getting to Yes: Negotiating Agreement Without Giving In*, 3rd ed. (Penguin, 2011).

21   Dean Pruitt, 'Achieving Integrative Agreements', cited in Max Bazerman and Roy Lewicki, *Negotiating in Organizations* (SAGE Publications, Inc., 1983), pp. 35–37

22   Roger Fisher and William Ury, *Getting to Yes: Negotiating Agreement Without Giving In*, 3rd ed. (New York: Penguin, 2011).

23   This is where we can feel the blessed pinch of being a follower of Jesus (Matthew 5:11, 1 Peter 4:4, 2 Corinthians 12:10). God is always there to help though. Daniel is a great example; when he didn't want to cross his conscience, God opened up a way for him, at great risk, to walk with integrity (Daniel 1:8–20).

24   Max H. Bazerman and Don A. Moore, *Judgement in Managerial Decision Making*, 8th ed. (Wiley, 2012); Max H. Bazerman and Margaret Neale, 'Nonrational escalation of commitment in negotiation', *European Management Journal*, 10, no. 2 (1992):163–168.

25   Danny Miller, *The Icarus Paradox: How Exceptional Companies Bring About Their Own Downfall* (Harper, 1990).

26   Phil Knight, *Shoe Dog: A Memoir by the Creator of NIKE* (Scribner, 2016).

27   Michael E. Porter, *Competitive Strategy: Techniques for Analysing Industries and Competitors* (Free Press, 2004).

28   Timothy Keller in *The Reason for God: Belief in an Age of Scepticism* (Hodder & Stoughton, 2009) notes how the story has been used to try to reduce Christianity to just one explanation of a much broader God. He helpfully points out the arrogance in that stance; it suggests the onlooker has the perfect sight of the elephant and everyone else is blind.

29   Robert H. Waterman, Thomas J. Peters, Julien R. Phillips, 'Structure is not organization', *Business Horizons*, 23, no. 3 (1980).

30   Jürgen Radel, 'A Change Management Framework and the McKinsey 7S Model', HTW Berlin, 2020, youtube.com/watch?v=xz69ZHbWZ5k.

31   Everett M. Rogers, *Diffusion of Innovations, 5th ed.* (Free Press, 2003).

SECTION 4: LEADING CHURCH LIFE

1   *Luther's Works*, Vol. 34, "Career of the Reformer IV" (Concordia Publishing House, 1960), p.336.

2   Vance Christie, 'Gaining Assurance of Salvation – Susanna Wesley', *vancechristie.com*, 2 February 2017, vancechristie.com/2017/02/02/gaining-assurance-salvation-susanna-wesley.

3   Geoff Thomas, 'The Conversion of Charles Haddon Spurgeon: January 6, 1850', *Banner of Truth*, 1 January 2000, banneroftruth.org/uk/resources/articles/2000/the-conversion-of-charles-haddon-spurgeon-january-6-1850.

4   John Piper, *Finally Alive: What Happens When We Are Born Again?* (Christian Focus, 2009).

5   Dean Karnazes, *Ultramarathon Man: Confessions of an All-Night Runner* (Allen & Unwin, 2017).

6   J. Scott Duvall and J. Daniel Hays, *Grasping God's Word* (Zondervan, 2005).

7   Thomas. W. Manson, ed., *A Companion to the Bible* (Edinburgh, 1939), p.251.

8   Muriel Rukeyser, *The Speed of Darkness* (Vintage Books, 1971).

9   George Eldon Ladd, *The Gospel of the Kingdom: Scriptural Studies in the Kingdom of God* (Eerdmans, 1990).

10   Stephen Nichols, 'The Life and Legacy of Dietrich Bonhoeffer', 7 February 2022, *Crossway*, crossway.org/articles/podcast-the-life-and-legacy-of-dietrich-bonhoeffer-stephen-nichols.

11   Dietrich Bonhoeffer, *Dietrich Bonhoeffer Works Volume 9: The Young Bonhoeffer 1918–1927* (Fortress Press, 2002), p.363.

12   Haddon Robinson, *Biblical Preaching: The Development and Delivery of Expository Messages* (Baker Academic, 2014), p.119.

13   Charles H. Spurgeon, *The Complete Works of C. H. Spurgeon, Volume 66: Autobiography – Diaries, Letters, and Records* Vol. 1 (Delmarva Publications, 2015), chapter 12.

14   Robinson, *Biblical Preaching*, p.27.

15   Sam Chan, *Evangelism in a Skeptical World: How to Make the Unbelievable News about Jesus More Believable* (Zondervan, 2018).

16   Ronald Boyd-MacMillan, *Explosive Preaching: Letters on Detonating the Gospel in the 21st Century* (Paternoster, 2006).

17   Timothy Keller, *Preaching: Communicating Faith in a Sceptical Age* (Hodder & Stoughton, 2015).

18   Joseph R. Myers, *The Search to Belong: Rethinking Intimacy, Community, and Small Groups* (Zondervan, 2003).

19   For more information about missional communities see, vergenetwork.org/2014/11/13/what-is-a-missional-community.

20   Myers, *The Search to Belong*.

21   Alex Absalom and Bobby Harrington, *Discipleship That Fits: The Five Kinds of Relationships God Uses to Help Us Grow* (Zondervan, 2016).

22   George W. Bullard, Jr., *Pursuing the Full Kingdom Potential of Your Congregation, TCP Leadership Series* (Chalice Press, 2006).

23   Rick Warren, '6 Ways to Prevent Vision Drift in Your Church', *pastors.com*, 4 September 2018, pastors.com/6-ways-to-prevent-vision-drift-in-your-church.

24   'In his detailed survey of 1,700 churches, David Voas found that 64 percent of churches with a clear mission and purpose were growing but only 26 percent of churches without one were.' Bob Jackson, *What Makes Churches Grow?* (Church House Publishing, 2015), p.75.

25   Tim Dowley, ed., *Introduction to the History of Christianity*, 3rd ed. (Fortress Press, 2018).

26   Bruce L. Shelley, *Church History in Plain Language* (W Publishing Group, 1982).

27   marcusbennettlifecoach.co.uk.

28   John Travis, 'The C1 to C6 Spectrum: A Practical Tool for Defining Six Types of "Christ-centered Communities" Found in the Muslim Context', *Evangelical Missions Quarterly*, 1998, pp. 407–408.

29   John Finney, *Emerging Evangelism* (Darton, Longman and Todd, 2004), p.94.

30   Observed at my trip to Manchester City's Etihad Stadium in 2012.

31   See James K. A. Smith, *Desiring the Kingdom: Worship, Worldview, and Cultural Formation* (Baker Academic, 2009); and Doug Ponder, 'The Temple and the Shopping Mall', ReSource, 21 May 2016, remnantresource.org/the-temple-and-the-shopping-mall-worship.

32   Timothy Keller, *Center Church: Doing Balanced, Gospel-Centered Ministry in Your City* (Zondervan, 2012), p.89.

33   Mark Sayers, *A Non-Anxious Presence: How a Changing and Complex World Will Create a Remnant of Renewed Christian Leaders* (Moody Publishers, 2022).

34   'Postman hoards 20,000 letters in Germany', *Mail & Guardian*, 10 September 2008, mg.co.za/article/2008-09-10-postman-hoards-20nbsp000-letters-in-germany.

Diagram Credits

All copyrighted diagrams not original to Andy Frost and Chris Frost are used by permission and are the property of the respective copyright holders.

SECTION 1: LEADING YOURSELF

The Cycle of Grace © Trevor Hudson and Jerry P. Haas, *The Cycle of Grace: Living in Sacred Balance* (Upper Room Books, 2013).

The Handy Prayer Tool © Rick Warren (Daily Hope), pastorrick.com/how-to-use-your-hands-to-pray.

The Emotional Energy Matrix © Catherine McCarthy, Jean Gomes, and Tony Schwartz, *The Way We're Working Isn't Working: The Four Forgotten Needs That Energize Great Performance* (Simon & Schuster UK, 2016).

The Iceberg of Emotional Health © Peter Scazzerò, *Emotionally Healthy Spirituality* (Harper Colins Christian Publishing, 2011).

The Emotions Wheel © Leadskill, leadskill.com/feelings-wheel.

The Sweet Spot © Jim Collins, *Good to Great; Why Some Companies Make the Leap … And Others Don't* (Harper Collins, 2001).

SECTION 2: LEADING OTHERS

The Kübler-Ross Change Curve © Elisabeth Kübler-Ross, *On Death and Dying* (Simon & Schuster, 1969).

The Passive Listening Curve © Creative Realities, Inc., creativerealities.com/innovationist-blog/bid/43059/Ideation-Skills-The-Trouble-with-Passive-Listening.

The Drama Triangle © Stephen B. Karpman, *A Game Free Life. The definitive book on the Drama Triangle and Compassion Triangle by the originator and author. The new transactional analysis of intimacy, openness, and happiness* (Drama Triangle Publications, 2014).

The Circles of Control © Stephen Covey, *The 7 Habits of Highly Effective People* (Simon & Schuster, 2020).

Mehrabian's Formula of Communication, diagram based on Dr Albert Mehrabian's '7–38–55% Communication Rule' in Laura Handley, 'Business Change and Communication: Do words matter when building trust?', *RedWizard*, redwizard.consulting/business-change-and-communication-do-words-matter-when-building-trust.

Feedback Loops, diagram based on Jordan Peterson's concepts in *12 Rules for Life: An Antidote to Chaos* (Penguin, 2019).

Kurt Lewin's Group Dynamics © Bruce W. Tuckman and Mary Ann C. Jensen, 'Stages of Small-Group Development Revisited', *Group & Organization Studies*, Vol. 2(4), (Sage Publications Inc., 1977, pp. 419–427).

The Five Dysfunctions of a Team © Patrick Lencioni, *The Five Dysfunctions of a Team: A Leadership Fable* (J–B Lencioni Series); 1st ed. (John Wiley & Sons, 2002).

Humble, Hungry and Smart © Patrick Lencioni, *The Ideal Team Player: How to Recognize and Cultivate The Three Essential Virtues* (Wiley, 2016).

Kelley's Five Followership Styles © R. Kelley, *The Power of Followership: How to Create Leaders People Want to Follow and Followers Who Lead Themselves* (Bantam Dell, 1992).

SECTION 3: LEADING PROJECTS

Axelrod's Meeting Canoe © Dick and Emily Axelrod, *Let's Stop Meeting Like This* (Berrett-Koehler, 2014).

The Communication Strategy Continuum © Phillip G. Clampitt, *Communicating for Managerial Effectiveness* (Sage Publications, 2011).

Kahneman's System 1 and 2 Thinking, diagram based on Daniel Kahneman's concepts in *Thinking, Fast and Slow* (Penguin, 2012).

The Scenario Framework, diagram based on Woody Wade's concepts in *Scenario Planning: A Field Guide to the Future* (Wiley, 2012).

The Zone of Possible Agreement, diagram based on Max Bazerman and Margaret Neale's concepts in 'Nonrational escalation of commitment in negotiation', *European Management Journal*, Vol. 10(2), 1992.

Michael Porter's Five Forces © Michael E. Porter, *Competitive Strategy: Techniques for Analysing Industries and Competitors* (Simon & Schuster, 1979), simonandschuster.co.uk/books/The-Competitive-Strategy/Michael-E-Porter/9780743260886.

McKinsey's 7-S Framework © Robert H. Waterman Jr. and Tom Peters, *In Search Of Excellence: Lessons from America's Best-Run Companies* (Profile Books, 2015).

The Innovation Adoption Curve © Everett M. Rogers, *Diffusions of Innovations* (Free Press, 2003).

SECTION 4: LEADING CHURCH LIFE

The Interpretative Journey © J. Duvall and J. Hays, *Grasping God's Word* (Zondervan, 2001).

Kingdom Already but Not Yet, diagram based on George Eldon Ladd's concepts in, *Gospel of the Kingdom: Scriptural Studies in the Kingdom of God* (Eerdmans, 2011).

The Life Cycle and Stages of Congregational Development © George Bullard, *Pursuing the Full Kingdom Potential of Your Congregation* (Chalice Press, 2005).

Denomination Family Tree © Lisa Delay, lisadelay.com/blog/tag/family-tree-of-god-chart.

Snakes and Ladders © Marcus Bennett, marcusbennett.co.uk.

The Contextualisation Staircase, diagram based on John Travis, 'The C1 to C6 Spectrum: A Practical Tool for Defining Six Types of "Christ-centered Communities" Found in the Muslim Context', *Evangelical Missions Quarterly*, 1998, pp. 407–408.

Four Relationships, diagram based on Krish Kandiah's concepts in *Sharing Jesus: How to Put Your Faith into Words* (HOPE and Share Jesus International).

The Gather Movement Model © Gather Movement, gathermovement.org.

Printed in Great Britain
by Amazon

23466189R00137